Thongs or Flip-Flops?
Australian kids overseas
and what comes next

Tanya Crossman and Kath Williams

First Published in the United Kingdom in 2024 by Summertime Publishing

ISBN: 978-1-915264-05-3

Design by: Cath Brew
drawntoastory.com

Disclaimer
For confidentiality, some names have been changed.

This is a must-read for Aussie TCKs! It is well-researched, with plenty of input from those who at some stage in life have struggled to call Australia home. The helpful advice, relatable stories, and practical helps, serve to bridge what is a formidable chasm.

Stewart Hunt
National Director, Interserve Australia

◆◆◆

Having worked in international schools on four continents, and with three TCK dual-citizen Australian children of my own, I can say that I wish *Thongs or Flip Flops?* had been published earlier! It contains a wealth of information and practical advice for those returning to Australia and offers a refreshingly inclusive perspective on belonging. There are many ways of being Australian, as the unique and heartfelt experiences shared in this book demonstrate, and there's room for all of us!

Dr. Caroline Brokvam
Principal, International School of Western Australia

◆◆◆

It is likely that a Third Culture Kid (TCK) inhabits every classroom and every community in Australia. Are they flourishing or are they floundering, and what is a TCK anyway? Using the power of story, along with extensive research and personal experience, Tanya and Kath have written a uniquely Australian guide for teachers, parents and TCKs themselves. All Australian schools and public libraries need this easy-to-read but profoundly informative and insightful book on their shelves.

Sandra Scott
Global Connect Ambassador

◆◆◆

Defence families are highly mobile, so living overseas can be viewed as just another posting. Likewise, people can assume that those previous postings will adequately prepare a family to live in another country. It is heartwarming to have this resource that will help Defence kids understand what they experience abroad and hopefully extend them that validation they are seeking when they return.

Sam Gregory
FOCUS Military Ministry (Australian Defence Force Academy),
9 years parenting an Australian Military Kid

♦♦♦

Tanya and Kath have a deep understanding of Australian life, providing factual information about living in the country, whilst also sharing practical tips and tricks on how to navigate the cultural and structural realities of moving home. *Thongs or Flip-Flops?* is dedicated to those raising their family overseas and who are thinking about, or who are in the process of, their transition back 'home'. As an Australian parent of three TCKs living among worlds, and an international educator who has taught in six countries on four continents, I can highly recommend this invaluable addition to the literature.

Stephen Toole
M.Ed, educator (27 years);
currently an international school counsellor.

♦♦♦

Thongs or Flip-Flops? makes visible and gives a voice to the domain of issues that can complicate childhood through the experience of navigating the expat environment and returning to their passport country. The book's beauty is in the interweaving of the diverse voices of Australian TCKs, pithy observations from industry experts, along with the authors' compassionate messaging. It is a helpful resource that prompts reflection and discussion across significant topics that previously remained invisible and unheard. While the opportunities of growing up cross-culturally can be a great benefit to a person's formation, the cross-cultural experience also profoundly impacts a young person's development. *Thongs or Flip-Flops?* is written with lots of pragmatic suggestions and explanation so that key ideas are accessible. Tanya and Kath's inclusion of significant social moments (e.g. Australian humour, the importance of sport, and gift giving) make the read fun and perceptive. This book packs a punch at its end with guides for participating as an Australian citizen and points to resources for continued learning. Tanya and Kath, thank you for taking the time to love our TCKs through your listening, your giving honour and language to their experiences, and your sensitive compilation of several central themes.

Steph Schwarz
Registered Psychologist, Resilience Lead for SIM International

◆◆◆

There are numerous books around about TCKs, but *Thongs or Flip-Flops?* gives a much-needed perspective for those who are from, or attached to, Australia. We have two 'Aussie' daughters who were born in two different overseas countries and lived away from Australia for most of their childhood. As I read through the book I oscillated from thinking 'that would have been great for them to have known' and 'I wish my wife and I had known that!' The way it addresses the theoretical and practical gives a refreshingly balanced and informative perspective for TCKs who in some way call Australia 'Home'. The heartfelt testimonies capture their experience as kids and adults. As a parent of TCKs and mission leader, I learnt new things and now understand concepts I have heard about previously. *Thongs or Flip-Flops?* is an excellent resource for TCKs and their parents; it will make you laugh, cry, and reflect on the unique aspect of life as an Aussie TCK.

Malcolm Watts
National Director, SIM Australia

◆◆◆

Thongs or Flip-Flops? has a strong focus on self-compassion, patience, and the importance of inner strength. This book illuminates the path to lasting well-being during the reintegration process to Australia. Through the compelling stories and expert insights, the authors shine a light on the intricacies of being visible and invisible in the cultures abroad and in Australia. Effective strategies and suggestions provided make it an indispensable resource for those moving home and also for non-Australians in international school settings who may wish to understand their Australian students' or co-workers' ethos, colloquialisms and culture.

Kelly Somerville
Educator (20 years), most recently Assistant Head for Diversity and Development at Australian International School, Singapore (AIS)

◆◆◆

Thongs or Flip-Flops? is a book for the Australian soul, to look within yourself and make sense of what being an Australian means to you, no matter where in the world you are or what you are influenced by. This book offers you the tools and space to confront the thoughts you might be pushing to the back of your mind. You can love two places. You do not need to identify with just one, and that's okay! They will have different types of love. They each have their space in your heart! I love this book; it helps you pinpoint your thoughts and answer questions you have not yet asked of yourself, bringing so much clarity to your identity, which in turn brings inner peace.

Robyn Vogels
Owner of Plan4Australia,
International Relocation Specialist and Author

◆◆◆

What an amazing reference for Australians living overseas. *Thongs or Flip Flops?* doesn't shy away from saying it as it is, covering all aspects of life in and outside of Australia. As the mother of two young Aussie TCKs born in India who have never lived in Australia, I found this a comprehensive look at the issues and challenges our girls may face in the future. As I considered each of these challenges, I loved that I am supported by very sage advice and tips. In particular, Tanya and Kath's description of Inclusive Patriotism was enlightening; 26th January is an interesting day in our home – Australia Day and India's Independence Day. This book belongs in the home of all Australians living overseas.

Emily Rogers
Transition & Leadership Coach, The Leap To Lead

◆◆◆

Thongs or Flip-Flops? is an inspiring collection of reflections by TCKs with all kinds of cross-cultural life, study and work experience. Their voices will warm and delight, confront and surprise. I reckon the advice and tips from Tanya and Kath for Aussies living overseas are gold. This book will be a must-read for all Pioneers members from now on! Do yourself and any TCKs you know a favour by reading it.

Simon Longden
National Director, Pioneers Australia

◆◆◆

Tanya and Kath's book is a really useful compendium of experiences, understandings and guidance for all Australian TCKs. It's packed full of facts about Australian life and culture. I love the first-hand accounts! Such a good way to normalise the complex emotions TCKs feel. I just wish I'd had this book when I was a teenager and was able to hand it to the 'foreign students' I was a buddy to at school. It would have helped them enormously!

Cath Brew
Global LGBTQIA+ Inclusion Consultant and Coach

◆◆◆

I've lived outside of Australia for 38 years, in five different countries and cultures. Now in my early 60s, having not been back to Australia for 10 years, I was curious to read *Thongs or Flip-Flops?* and ultimately found myself engrossed. The chapters on repatriation and understanding Australian culture were especially eye-opening. Although I proudly identify with my passport country, Australia, it became clear that if I were to repatriate, I'd be returning to my country as a 'foreigner'! For anyone who has lived outside of Australia, is planning to live outside of Australia, or is returning to live in Australia, read this book! It offers vital information, particularly for parents, teachers, counsellors, and anyone supporting TCKs and Australians repatriating.

Louise Ross
Writer and podcaster (books include *The Winding Road to Portugal* and *Women Who Walk*)

◆◆◆

To all Australians who grew up globally, all around the world, including those who shared their experiences with us during the writing of this book.

Your stories are valid and valuable.

Contents

Acknowledgements

Tanya

My first acknowledgement is Joshua Haller – the partner I love collaborating with and working with, even when we are forced oceans apart. Always better together.

My family on three continents have been very supportive of my work – even when they didn't understand it! To the Crossmans, Hochguertels, Mavecs, Godbys, Sue Nicholas, Zee-Hallers, Hubbards, Coyles, McNeices, Nacos, Keith and Lesley – you are my people, and I am thankful for you all. Finally, always in my heart are Simon, Nathan, and Harry: you believed in me even if you didn't always 'get' what I did, and I carry you with me.

I also want to acknowledge Aussies I have been friends with over the decades I've spent outside Australia – even those I'm rarely/never in touch with anymore. First up – to the social group of Australian IBM-ers in the tri-state area back in 1996–1997: thank you for being an oasis for a stressed out teen TCK. Also, thanks to friends who added some Aussie flavour to my adult years abroad: Mel, Elinor, Anita, Jo, Barry and Tina, Bruce and Audrey, Geoff and Yvonne, Andersons, Bec W, Hills, Lyons, Sharee and Nathaniel, Nick B, Ruth and Jono, Craig H, Jagelmans, Applebys, Litchfields, Chris B, Nathaniel C, Willsmores, Lepelaars, and all the others who have shared global Aussie space with me!

Big thanks go to the team at TCK Training. I love working with you all and collaborating with people who share my passion for helping Third Culture Kids thrive throughout their lives. Thanks also to the Summertime team, for helping bring to life so many resources that support globally mobile families – including both my first book and this one.

Kath

There are so many people to thank for their investment and contributions that have made a difference in my life.

My parents, Pat and Bruce Williams, and my brother Scott: for always believing in me and knowing that I can do things and for always investing in me.

For my Aussie TCKs, who have helped me to have an understanding of what it is for an Aussie TCK to come back into Australia. They have been on the journey from the very beginning: Joshua, David, Daniel Lohmeyer, Anna, Jess and Felicity Townsend, Tennyson and Elliot Litchfield, Sheena and Thalia, the Willsmore Clan (Jesse, Izzy, Caleb, Peter, Emma, Lauren, and Tessa), Rachel Johnson, Jess Meyers, Chris and Emily Bowman, Jeni Ward, Frances Early, and many more. Thanks for letting me be a part of your community and listen to your stories, cry with you when you have needed me, and just be there for you as you journey to Australia.

My organisation, who have seen my passion for TCKs to be well cared for, for their investment in me, and their encouragement: Jane Fairweather, Christine Gobius, Jenny Goddard, and Norm Tucker.

For all my supporters and friends who have financially and prayerfully supported me over the past 10 years: I couldn't do the work I do without you and without your support.

Foreword

It was back in 2014 when our paths first crossed. A phone call from a mutual friend (shout out to John Sorrell) enticed me to meet Tanya with the words, "You two speak the same language." Was he talking about our Australian accents? Was he talking about our shared passion for supporting and empowering students crossing cultures? Over coffee on the upper floor of a Singaporean shophouse, I discovered it was both.

Tanya was en route from China to her passport country, Australia, with the aim of furthering her studies and completing the publication of her first book, *Misunderstood*. Having witnessed first-hand the impact of unmanaged mobility on learning and relationships in my international school classrooms, I had recently left a fulfilling role as a classroom teacher to embark on a new career as an educational consultant to schools and families, specialising in student cross-cultural transitions. Beneath a rickety rattan ceiling fan and surrounded by the gentle sway of humid air, we shared stories of our own experiences of crossing cultures and found synergies in our observations of the effects of global mobility on the youth in our care. Woven throughout our conversation was a golden thread of both responsibility and calling, drawing on our connections with Australia, working with Third Culture Kids (TCKs), their families, those who educate them and our desire to equip them to effectively navigate the triumphs and trials associated with living and learning among cultures. It's a thread that continues to bind our professional lives and now includes Kath, creating a colourful tapestry providing comfort, comprehension, connection, and confidence to many TCKs, families and educational staff around the world – including Australia.

Speaking of Australia, this book is what TCKs with connections 'Down Under' (Australian TCKs), and those who care for them, have been looking for! As I read each page it was like holding up a mirror to many of my family's experiences and the stories I hear from my clients, over and over again. I feel certain that the candour, authenticity and humour conveyed in this book will be like holding up a mirror for many TCKs too. There is power in reframing transitions so that we're looking from the perspective of those actually making the transition, because there are important insights to be gained into our understanding, care and practices as TCKs, educators, parents, caregivers and sponsoring organisations. Throughout *Thongs or Flip Flops?* Tanya and Kath give a voice to Australian TCKs. A voice that has been largely unheard in the literature to date. A voice that can and should inform our policies, practices and perspectives.

This book, as the authors mention, is a companion resource, to be read alongside other TCK resources. I wish this book had been my companion when my family and I were preparing to return 'home' to Australia after years of living in South East Asia. I also wish it had been my companion as I moved throughout Australia as a child of a domestically mobile family. Danielle's comments about accents in *Chapter 7* could have prepared me for the variety of accents within and across state borders. Who knew that c-aa-stle and c-ar-stle were the same word or bathers and cozzies meant the same thing? The Glossary of Australian vocabulary would have been a life saver for me, and later for my children as they navigated their re-entry transition. We left these shores with the understanding we were departing Australia but returned to discover our passport country had been renamed to 'Straya! I wish I had Lucy's words of encouragement in *Chapter 5* to accompany me during our repatriation, reminding my family and me to foster our attitude of curiosity. I wish our friends and family had had this book to help them understand the challenges each of our family members was working through after the frenzy of 'Welcome Home' events and before we could honestly say, "I feel settled here." I wish I had been able to give this book to the staff at my children's school. Perhaps then, instead of rolling their eyes when my sons couldn't immediately identify where Canberra was located on a map of Australia or what the emblems on the NSW flag represented or what year Captain Cook invaded Australia, the teachers would have gone beyond the Australian accent and the tanned skin to tap into their story, knowledge and experiences, uncovering gems such as where the Strait of Malacca is located and why it is so important in the global economy, which flag represents Malaysia and the significance of the symbols and colours which adorn it or a sensory description of the labyrinth of tunnels where the British capitulation of Singapore took place. I wish I could have shared this book with every Australian university admissions team member, residential college staff member and counsellor as I equipped TCKs for tertiary study in Australia, to help them understand the differences and similarities between the TCK experience, the international student experience, and the domestic student experience, to shine a spotlight on the remarkable cultural bridges they have in their midst. I hope that my wishes become your reality.

When it comes to reality, I particularly appreciate the structure of *Thongs or Flip Flops?* Each chapter outlines the challenges associated with mobility across cultures, which are then followed by opportunities and suggested strategies for overcoming or navigating those challenges. As Doug Ota, founder of Safe Passage Across Networks (SPAN), says, "Mobility across cultures can be one of the richest sources of learning and personal growth that life has to offer. But these benefits are only likely to occur when mobility's massive challenges are managed well."

Both Tanya and Kath have brought their extensive life experiences to this book (don't skip the Acknowledgements and Introduction!) to provide a resource which can positively contribute to managing mobility so the reader can indeed reap the benefits of a globally mobile life. People develop and learn best when they feel seen, supported, and safe. Remember the mirror I mentioned? *Thongs or Flip Flops?* opens the door for Australian TCKs to be seen like never before, to be supported more comprehensively and to feel safe as they unpack their own experiences and cultural identity to become authentically known. Our world is one where 258 million people are living outside their country of origin for a variety of reasons. That's 3.4% of humanity. We can no longer expect individuals to fit into traditional mono-cultural ways of defining belonging and identity. The conclusion of this book speaks to the heart of Australian TCKs. It is my hope that you will embrace the authors' words, feeling the freedom to choose what Australia means to you and how this is woven together with your other cultural threads to create your own unique tapestry. It is not either/or. It can be both/and. A bit like pavlova really!

Alongside my experiences as a 30+ year veteran in the field of education, a mum to two Australian TCKs, a daughter of a domestically mobile family, and a survivor of a somewhat rocky repatriation to Australia, I bring many tools to my work as a Youth Intercultural Transitions Specialist at Globally Grounded and Director of Training and Consulting at Safe Passage Across Networks (SPAN). I am so excited to now have *Thongs or*

Flip Flops? as an additional tool in my Transitions Toolkit as I continue to work with schools and families within and beyond our Aussie shores. It is a comprehensive and much-needed resource for Australians who have lived or are living overseas, and all those who educate and care for them. I highly recommend this book be added to your Transitions Toolkit too.

I hope you enjoy reading it as much as I enjoy lamingtons and Vegemite!

Jane Barron
Youth Intercultural Transitions Specialist, Globally Grounded
Director of Training & Consulting, Safe Passage Across Networks (SPAN)

Before You Begin

This is a book written by Australians who have lived outside Australia, for Australians who are living, or have lived, outside Australia. We don't expect you to know everything about Australia, including the words Australians use, the things Australians do, and what is considered 'normal' or 'typical' in Australia. This book is a safe space for people who are Australian 'on paper' but don't always (or ever) feel it.

Australian Language

In the back of this book you'll find a glossary of Australian words. Any word we use in this book that is used mostly by Australians (or means something different in Australia) is marked with an asterisk* to let you know you can find a definition in the glossary.

Australian Geography

When talking about Australia's six states and two main territories, we will generally use the commonly accepted abbreviations. Here is a list for your reference, along with the state capitals:

The States
1. New South Wales (NSW), Sydney
2. Queensland (QLD), Brisbane
3. South Australia (SA), Adelaide
4. Tasmania (TAS), Hobart
5. Victoria (VIC), Melbourne
6. Western Australia (WA), Perth

The Territories
1. The Australian Capital Territory (ACT), Canberra
2. The Northern Territory (NT), Darwin

Currency

All prices/costs in the book are in Australian dollars (AUD).

Introduction

When I (Tanya) was 13 years old, my dad's company transferred him to the USA – and along with him, my mum, me, and my two younger sisters. For two years we attended local public schools in Connecticut, the only Australians our classmates had ever met. Once every month or so, we connected with other Australians working for the same company – we'd hang out, eat pavlova*, play cricket*. I had a friend from Northern Ireland, transferred by her mum's company. Other than that, I was immersed in American life. Two years later, I was excited to 'go home' where I would be 'normal'. Except when I got back to Australia, it turned out my accent had shifted (along with my fashion sense), and my new peers nicknamed me 'Miss America'.

That is a snapshot of what it can be like to be an Australian child experiencing international life. Moving countries with the intent (immediate or eventual) to return to your passport country is called expatriation, and the people who do this are expatriates (expats for short). People who grow up this way, who have this experience during childhood, are called Third Culture Kids (TCKs). Common sectors where this occurs include foreign affairs, defence, missionaries, international companies, and international educators.

I (Kath) grew up in Australia but had multiple friends throughout my childhood who were from immigrant or missionary families. I learned from them that Australian cultural and linguistic quirks were hard to understand and pick up. I also saw it was hard for kids returning to Australia. I learned the term Third Culture Kid in 2013 but it was in 2016, when I began living in Cambodia and mentoring TCKs there, that the meaning really sank in for me. I fell in love with these young people. I wanted to help them adjust to Australian life and have a smooth re-entry.

If you are new to the terminology of Third Culture Kids, please don't be worried! I (Tanya) lived the experience without hearing the term until my mid-twenties, and I (Kath) knew and cared for many TCKs before knowing the term. Whatever you do or don't know about TCKs, this book is for you, and we will explain it all in the following pages, we promise.

1

There are lots of great resources for Third Culture Kids out there. Tanya even wrote one of them! This book is not intended to replace any of those. It is instead a companion resource. We imagine Australians living overseas, as well as their families and caregivers, using this book alongside their favourite general TCK resource/s. (We share a long list of excellent TCK resources we recommend at the back of the book – including Tanya's book *Misunderstood*.)

This book shares information that is specific to the Australian TCK experience. It centres on the Australian context, which is so different to most other places and cultures. We share specific cultural and practical information to help Australian TCKs find their way upon return and as adults – from attending a barbie or dealing with Centrelink to marriage and children in the future – whether they choose to live in Australia or elsewhere in the world.

The book is full of stories from Australian TCKs reflecting on their experiences and their identity as Australians. Each story is followed by their name (most are pseudonyms), their age now, how many years they lived outside Australia before the age of 18, and the broad reason their family moved overseas. Some were with the Department of Foreign Affairs and Trade (DFAT) or the Australian Defence Force (ADF). Others were sent abroad for business or to work with a humanitarian/development organisation. Some were missionaries, some were teachers (often in international schools) or studying as adults, and some families had reasons other than work – such as living in their other passport country.

This book does *not* have all the answers. There are other books, more comprehensive books, that tell more of the TCK story (like those in the *Resources* list). What this book does – that no other book does – is tell the stories of Australian TCKs, what it means to be Australian in the world, and what it feels like to be an Australian coming 'home' to an unfamiliar country.

Being Australian

There are hundreds of ways to be Australian.

Introduction

It can be something you absorb through being raised in Australia, or by an Australian family. Or perhaps while your citizenship is a fact, being 'Australian' is something that you don't feel – a country to which you have little emotional connection. It might be something you want, something to which you cling. It might be something you aren't interested in, or actively disconnect from. It might be an identity you slowly develop over years, or decades.

Here's how some of the Australian TCKs we interviewed described their relationship with Australia:

> *Being Australian is more of a formality than a personal connection.*
> Mei Mei, 22
> – 10 years with a missionary organisation

> *Ultimately, living here has been great. Melbourne being so multicultural and so diverse is really cool. I love that. But I don't like being Australian – I don't like being a part of colonisation.*
> Cardamon, 23
> – 11 years in aid and development

> *I like Australia as a place. I have gratitude toward the country but don't feel allegiance or belonging to it.*
> Elliot, 25
> – 11 years with a missionary organisation

> *My relationship with Australia is complex and has evolved over time. At 18, Australia was just my passport country and where my parents lived. With time and travel I came to appreciate my Australian identity and now proudly call Australia home. That said, parts of me still belong elsewhere.*
> Nathan, 28
> – 5 years with a missionary organisation

> **"**
> *It took me a long time to be at peace with being Australian; to recognise the reality that I am (primarily) Australian, and that Australia is the place where I have the most cultural capital. An enduring effect of my TCK experience is a reluctance to categorise myself as Australian, despite all the evidence to the contrary!*
> Matthew, 35
> – 9 years with a missionary organisation

> **"**
> *Australia is somewhere where I lived as a child. At this point, I don't feel Australian.*
> Christina, 59
> – 13 years in the business sector

Being an Australian citizen – being a citizen of any country – comes with both rights and responsibilities. We're going to talk about those in this book. More than that, though, we're going to talk about what it 'feels' like to be Australian – when you're outside Australia, when you re-enter Australia, when you're trying to fit in and when you feel like you don't.

There are mainstream Australian cultural norms, and it's helpful to understand these. For that reason, we'll talk about some things that are handy to know about life and socialising in Australia – such as easy topics of conversation, popular activities, and common missteps. That said, there is no specific mould you have to fit. There may be (almost certainly will be) expectations that others have for you, and probably some expectations you have for yourself, about what it means to be Australian. But *you* get to decide what being Australian means to you.

You may choose to adapt to the cultural norms of Australia as much as possible. You may choose to subvert those norms because you have different beliefs. Both of these are valid choices. We make similar choices in any country where we live.

Australia is not a monolith, but a multicultural country. According to the Australian Bureau of Statistics (ABS), 48% of Australian citizens have at least one parent born outside Australia, and 28% were born overseas. Mainstream culture is changing, and there are many different subcultures as well. As we talk about 'Australian culture' throughout this book, we do so knowing that we are talking in generalisations that do not apply to every person, every family, every community. That said, mainstream Anglo*-Australian culture still has a big impact on how most Australians move through society. Understanding the cultural norms of this space is helpful, even if you do not spend much time in it.

> 66
> *I didn't understand why my efforts to fit in weren't reciprocated and only later came to understand how much of a culture is opaque even to people who've grown up in it. The way Australian-ness is presented in society is that everybody can trace all their family back to the First Fleet*, and everybody's great-grandparents ran a sheep farm somewhere, and it's not true.*
> Fernando, 54
> – 2 years for family reasons

All your experiences – wherever in the world they happened – become part of you, and your Australian-ness. Living outside Australia means we see Australia differently. That is *not* a bad thing! Sometimes it causes a few bumps in relationships with other Aussies – that's normal, and we'll talk more about it later on – but your global perspective is a good thing you bring to your life in Australia.

> 66
> *I really benefited from time spent growing up outside Australia. I think the experience of seeing how people lived in developing countries made me see how much we take for granted in Australia. Friendships with people from other cultures changed the way I thought about popular culture in Australia. I think it protected me from wanting to fit in or mould myself to show an 'acceptable image' as an adult. I still feel grateful for the gift of not thinking everything we have here is normal.*
> Alice, 52
> – 8 years with DFAT

About Third Culture Kids

In addition to the resource list at the end of the book, it is important to start with a clear foundation of what we mean when we talk about Third Culture Kids.

TCKs generally

The term Third Culture Kid (TCK) dates back to research done in the 1950s and 1960s. An early form of the term appeared in a 1973 paper by Ruth Hill Useem, in the context of expatriate Americans working in India. David Pollock was a pioneer in the term's expansion to embrace all people who lived outside their passport countries during childhood, and its use became common among missionary researchers in the 1980s. Around the same time, Norma McCaig was using the term 'global nomad' with a similar definition. The touchstone explanation of Third Culture Kids came in the 1999 book by David Pollock and Ruth Van Reken, *Third Culture Kids: Growing Up Among Worlds.* In the book's third edition (published after David Pollock's death, with his son Michael Pollock as co-author), the following definition of a TCK is given:

> "A person who spends a significant part of his or her first 18 years of life accompanying parent(s) into a country that is different from at least one parent's passport country(ies) due to a parent's choice of work or advanced training."

In simple language, a Third Culture Kid is someone who lives outside their passport country as a child, usually because their parent's occupation initiated a family move. Generally speaking, the "significant part" of childhood is at least a year or two, but it could be their entire childhood. A TCK may never live in their passport country at all.

"
For the first 15 years after coming back to Australia, I felt abnormal. After hearing David Pollock speak in 1990, when I was about to get married and head overseas, I realised what I felt was actually normal for someone who had experienced growing up overseas. This was my 'aha' moment and was transformative in helping me to be content and resilient. Feeling different does still occur after almost 50 years but I know how to handle it.
David, 61
– 6 years in aid and development

"
Understanding some of what it means to be a TCK (this term wasn't used when I returned) has helped me own my story and start to feel comfortable in my own skin again. Something I feel has been absent since we returned.
Kaylee, 39
– 6 years with a missionary organisation

"
Being a white Australian in a white Australian family where my parents both grew up in and identify with Australia, I really struggled to work out why I didn't really feel like I belong here, when on the surface I really should 'fit in'. Discovering that there are more people who feel this way, who don't feel like they belong even though they 'should' is comforting. It makes me feel less alone – I've finally convinced myself that I'm not making it up.
Rosie, 25
– 6 years with DFAT

The three cultures referenced in the name 'Third' Culture Kid are now generally recognised to be types of cultures, not a count of the number of cultures an individual interacts with. I (Tanya) explain the three types of cultures this way in my book *Misunderstood*:

"The first culture is the Legal Culture – this is any country in which the child has legal standing: their passport country (or countries). This may also include having permanent residency in a country.... The second culture is the Geographic Culture – any culture in which the child has lived. This may or may not include their legal culture(s).... Both Legal and Geographic cultures contribute to a TCK's understanding of the world and how it works. TCKs may absorb elements of food, dress, pop culture, body language, values and manners from each culture, blending them into a unique personal style or applying them differently according to context.... The third culture is the Relational Culture. It is the culture of shared experiences – people who relate to each other because they have been through similar things. Many 21st century TCKs identify more strongly with people who have shared their childhood experiences than with those who have merely shared a location."

Australian TCKs will count Australia as a legal culture, but if they have citizenship or permanent residency in another country as well, they will have more than one legal culture. In international school classrooms I (Tanya) have visited around the world, about one-third of students had more than one legal culture. And in my research for *Misunderstood*, 40% of TCKs had four or more geographic cultures.

> **❝**
> *Despite experiencing life in another first-world country, very little was the same as my home continent. Despite also being a predominantly white, English-speaking, well-educated nation, words that could be used to also describe Australia, this new country was so vastly different.*
> Tayo, 21
> – 6 years with the ADF

TCKs are often influenced by multiple cultures – that is part of the shared experience of a Third Culture upbringing. Other shared experiences may include familiarity with travel, frequent transitions, friends moving away, and long-distance relationships with extended family. While there are wonderful opportunities that come with this life, there can also be difficulties.

> **❝**
> *Whilst I had some incredible experiences as a child, there were also some really traumatic experiences that I still haven't fully processed. These were to do with being almost the same, but too different to fit in properly, wherever I went. I'm grateful to my parents for affording us such fantastic opportunities as children; I just wish there was more support when we repatriated, as to this day I still don't feel like I fit in with other Australians.*
> Rosie, 25
> – 6 years with DFAT

My (Tanya's) book *Misunderstood* discusses the different experiences, perspectives, and emotions TCKs experience due to their multiple cultural influences. We highly recommend you read it and check out the *Resources* section at the back of this book for support when handling the tougher side of global mobility.

"
If you only lived in one other location for an extended period of time, it makes it hard to really feel like you can belong back in your passport country. Whatever age you return impacts your future experiences; there will always be part of you that is hard for others to understand and which prevents you from feeling fully Australian. It's difficult knowing that you can never go back to the life you had overseas but will also never truly fit in here.
Danielle, 19
– 11 years with a missionary organisation

"
Many years ago I returned to Australia. The feeling of being different has stayed with me for over 50 years. I'm glad beyond measure I lived overseas as a child but it has often made me look at life differently to my friends. The only people who understand are those who have experienced different cultures.
Liz, 68
– 10 years with a missionary organisation

Australian TCKs

For the purposes of this book, we define an Australian TCK as: anyone who, while holding Australian citizenship, and before the age of 18, lived outside Australia for at least one year.

An Australian TCK might have been born in Australia. They might not have been.

An Australian TCK might never have lived in Australia.

An Australian TCK might have lived all but a few years of their life in Australia.

An Australian TCK might have given up their Australian citizenship later in life.

An Australian TCK might hold more than one citizenship – and might always have done so.

An Australian TCK might have lived their early childhood in Australia, and their later childhood in another country (or countries).

An Australian TCK might have lived their early childhood outside Australia, before returning to Australia during their later childhood.

An Australian TCK might have an Australian accent, and they might not.

An Australian TCK might call Australia 'home', and they might not.

There are many ways to be an Australian TCK.

We surveyed 212 Australian TCKs about their experiences. We will call this group of Aussie TCKs 'our cohort' from here on. Our cohort ranged in age from 18–78, came from different backgrounds, had lived in different countries, and had varied experiences and feelings about those experiences. Throughout this book there are statistics and quotes from these TCKs, to show you a wide range of experiences – some similar to yours, some different. No matter what your experience has been like, you are not alone.

Our cohort was 67% female, 31% male, and 2% non-binary. 84% had lived in Australia both as children and as adults. 7% had not lived in Australia as children; 7.5% had not lived in Australia as adults. The remaining 1.5% had visited Australia, but had never lived here.

Most of our cohort (92%) had lived outside Australia as children due to their parents' work. 37% were with missionary organisations; 15% were teachers; 13% worked in aid and development; 4% were with the Australian Defence Force (ADF); and 2% were with the Department of Foreign Affairs and Trade (DFAT). Another 21% had other work, whether corporate transfers or simply working in other countries. Of those who had lived overseas not due to work, 2% were in education without being teachers (such as studying abroad), and 6% had other family reasons – mostly dual citizenship.

70% of our cohort were Gen Z or Millennials; the remaining 30% were older – with the oldest two born in 1944! The cohort lived outside Australia for different lengths of time as children. 8% lived outside

Australia for fewer than three years; 7% lived their entire childhood outside Australia. Five were born with a different citizenship and became Australian later in childhood; four of these were adopted from outside Australia. One in five were dual citizens, and seven had permanent residency in another country. One was no longer an Australian citizen. More than half said their Australian citizenship was very or extremely important to them.

Resources for Australian TCKs

There is a dearth of resources for TCKs in Australia. Families transferred abroad for their work in various industries have told us about the resources they wish they'd had, about feeling alone in their Australian repatriation, and about the long list of things they wished they'd known earlier. There are a few informal online networks, including groups for returning Australian citizens (these grew dramatically during the COVID-19 pandemic) and some groups for Adult TCKs in various cities across Australia (mostly run by missionary kids). The Australia-wide mission support organisation Missions Interlink provides some resources for Australian missionary kids. These include retreats, camps, and virtual workshops for parents and other caregivers.

66
There was lots of information and support for American TCKs, but I had to filter and adjust any advice I ever got to fit me because it never seemed to apply to my specific situation, which made me feel like I was never understood. That meant that my immediate family became really important because they were the only ones who understood. I'm incredibly grateful for my life and I wouldn't change anything about it, but it was pretty isolating at times.
Wren, 20
– 18 years with a missionary organisation

66
We had a lot of transition training in our international school but it was training TCKs for repatriation to an American context – not the Australian context. Everything I learned about repatriation came from my Australian parents.
Alex, 23
– 13 years with a missionary organisation

> **"**
> *We had little preparation for either the move over there or repatriation. I don't think our family or people around us understood the impact. It was just another posting – and an exciting one at that. What could go wrong? A lot, it turned out.*
> Shellie, 54
> – 1 year with the ADF

This lack of resources is a large driving force behind the writing of this book. No matter what networks you do or do not belong to, you deserve access to information about the experiences of Australian TCKs. Thousands of Australians have been through this experience before you and many of them can be found here, in these pages, to share their stories with you.

We will be discussing things that are specific to the Australian context, which don't show up in general TCK resources. This includes changing schools (and curriculums) mid-year, adjusting to Australian attitudes towards swearing and drinking, dealing with the anti-American sentiment common in Australia, and the Australian cultural value against arrogance. I (Tanya) returned to Australia as a teen 25 years ago. I have spent 18 years working with globally mobile families and 10 years writing for/about TCKs. Despite all this experience, some of the stories shared in this book made even *me* feel seen, heard, and understood – because I'd never seen these things explored in TCK literature before.

For parents taking children out of Australia, or already living abroad, we hope you gain insight into how this experience may affect your kids, and resources for how to support them well throughout their lives.

For those who have made the journey from international life to 'returning' to Australia, we hope you also experience that sense of being seen, heard, and understood as you read. For those of you who are looking ahead to living in Australia, may the stories of those who have gone before you light the way.

Section 1:
When You Live Overseas

Chapter 1:

Being Australian Overseas

Why I feel more Australian outside Australia

When I (Tanya) first moved outside Australia at 13 (to the USA), I suddenly felt *Australian* in a way I never had before. Since then I have continued to move back and forth between Australia and other countries. I have learned that the further I am from Australian communities, the more Australian I feel. That might sound strange, but it's actually really normal.

> **"**
> *Australia is a larger part of my identity when I am overseas than it is when I am in Australia. I suppose I define myself partially by being different to those around me.*
> Calvin, 23
> – 14 years with a missionary organisation

> **"**
> *Outside of Australia you are being compared to non-Australians, so you seem (and feel) much more Australian.*
> John, 28
> – 3 years with a missionary organisation

An Australian living in Australia is one of many. An Australian living overseas might be the only Australian in their classroom or workplace. They might be the only Australian family living on their street, or in their whole town. Being Australian makes you stand out, a way that people describe you. One-third of our cohort said they were often or always described as 'The Australian' while living overseas, whether as children or as adults.

> **"**
> *There were not many other Australians living in our country overseas and I was often known as 'the Australian one'. I clung more to my Australian traits there than within Australia.*
> Rebecca, 33
> – 5 years with a missionary organisation

As children living outside Australia, 14% of our cohort spent time with other Australians (other than their families) every day, but 36% saw other Australians less than once a month. 28% knew few or no Australians overseas. Nearly two-thirds were the only Australian in a group every day.

Those in our cohort who lived overseas as adults had even less contact with other Australians. Only 7% spent time with other Australians every day; 42% saw other Australians less than once a month; 40% knew maybe a few or no other Australians; 69% were the only Australian in a group daily. When you live like this, it's no wonder you *feel* more Australian outside Australia. It's a part of you that is constantly contrasted and even pointed out! When I (Tanya) attended a local high school in the USA, I was the only Australian in a school with 3,000 staff and students; every time I opened my mouth, people knew I was 'The Australian' – even if I'd never met them before.

Not only that, you may well be seen as an authority on all things Australia. You are probably asked questions about Australia – some may be quite repetitive; others might have you rolling your eyes a little.

> **"**
> *There were very few other Australians around so you are the expert by default. By being able to answer questions about Australia and laughing at ridiculous assumptions that we ride kangaroos, you feel more Australian than when surrounded by other Australians.*
> Danielle, 19
> – 11 years with a missionary organisation

> **"**
> *For many years I was the only Australian in my class. Whenever something came up about Australia, I would be asked to comment on it. But growing up overseas, I really didn't know much about Australia other than what my parents had taught me. I felt put on the spot and uncomfortable.*
> Alex, 23
> – 13 years with a missionary organisation

Then you land in Australia – and that defining characteristic doesn't define you anymore because *everyone* is Australian. Plus, you know less about daily life in Australia and Australian pop culture than anyone around you. So, of course you feel *less* Australian in Australia. It might be a common enough experience, but that doesn't make it any less disconcerting.

66
I really can't empathise with people who talk about growing up here and childhood memories and doing all the 'classic' Australian things. My friends describe their childhoods and I just can't relate.
Rosie, 25
– 6 years with DFAT

66
I didn't feel particularly Australian. It was where my mum was from (my dad is from a different country). I thought of nationality mostly in terms of geography. Even now part of me doesn't want to feel Australian.
Angela, 30
– 7 years with a missionary organisation

One thing that is important to note here is that this experience is not universal. Some struggle to be acknowledged as Australian due to the colour of their skin – both at home and away. Different Australian TCKs we spoke to, especially of different ages, had different experiences of this. Some found there was less of a struggle for acknowledgement of their Australian-ness inside Australia. Others found the racism of Australia to be so off-putting they did not want to identify as Australian. We will talk more about racism in Australia later, but it bears acknowledging right from the start.

66
The stereotypical Aussie is perceived to be white. One of the things I had to grapple with identifying as an Australian overseas was people not believing me or not thinking that I was a 'real' Aussie because I was not white.
Nathan, 28
– 5 years with a missionary organisation

Encountering stereotypes of Australia

Questions that make our eyes roll are often related to stereotypes people hold about Australia. Stereotypes are common everywhere. It's a shortcut, a way of judging a whole place or people in a few broad strokes. It's easy to do when you've never been to the place or met any of the people.

> **"**
>   *As a child, I lived in West Texas for eight years. Most people there didn't know what Australia was, much less where it was and what it was like.*
> Andrew, 34
> – 8 years for family reasons, 9 years in the education/business sectors

Four in five of our cohort were aware of stereotypes of Australia as children living overseas; one in five directly felt those stereotypes applied to them. Here are some of the stereotypes they encountered – that:

1. Australians have kangaroos/koalas as pets (59%)
2. Australians speak like Crocodile Dundee* (49%)
3. Australians are laidback people (41%)
4. Australians are descended from criminals (31%)
5. Australians live in the outback* (29%)
6. Australia is all beaches (26%)

Those in our cohort who lived overseas as adults were even more aware of Australian stereotypes, with 92% noticing them and 1 in 3 feeling them directly applied. The stereotypes they noticed included that:

1. Australians are laidback people (59%)
2. Australians speak like Crocodile Dundee* (56%)
3. Australians have kangaroos/koalas as pets (47%)
4. Australians are descended from criminals (46%)
5. Australians drink a lot of alcohol (41%)
6. Australians swear a lot (36%)
7. Australia is all beaches (31%)
8. Australians live in the outback* (28%)

> **❝**
> *Common stereotypes as Australians included having funny accents, riding kangaroos to school, the whole country being the outback*, and constantly being surrounded by dangerous reptiles.*
> Danielle, 19
> – 11 years with a missionary organisation

Many people we meet overseas have never been to Australia; their picture of Australia comes from what they have seen on TV or in movies. Perhaps that was *The Crocodile Hunter**, or tourism advertisements of pristine natural environments. Whatever picture they have in their head, it won't match reality. Sometimes, you are the first Australian they have met. Now you get to be part of their new stereotype of all Australians. No pressure!

One-third of our cohort said they sometimes or often exaggerated their Australian-ness in order to stand out overseas, whether as children or adults! Sometimes it went the other way.

> **❝**
> *We were one of a very few Australian families. I think most people liked Australians, and I was proud to be Australian, not American or Korean 'like everyone else'. But when I would come back to visit Australia, I'd always make sure I used my strongest American accent so Australians would know I was 'different'.*
> Sera, 34
> – 15 years with a missionary organisation

In this situation you can become a bit of a celebrity – for better and for worse. When you have your twentieth, or one hundredth, conversation about whether Australians speak English and have pet kangaroos, it is easy to get frustrated. It might be new to them but it is getting pretty old for you!

> **❝**
> *I wish people knew that there were different kinds of Australian accents. I had a pretty mild Sydney kind of accent; not everyone speaks like Steve Irwin*.*
> Lyndall, 30
> – 5 years for family reasons

That's not even counting the people who ask, or outright say, things that are offensive. Listening to jokes that all Australians are criminals because we are descended from convicts gets old quickly – even if, as in my (Tanya's) case, you do in fact have First Fleet* and Second Fleet* convicts in your family tree. Hearing offensive stereotyping of Australia's Indigenous people heaps insult on top of grievous injury.

Representing Australia

If you lived in a place where you were known as The Australian, or where your skin colour or accent set you apart, it's likely that you felt some sense of being seen – that what you did and said reflected on others, perhaps even on all of Australia.

> **"**
> *My siblings and I were the only Australians we knew for most of the 13 years we were over there. As the only link our friends had to Australia, we were the default experts on it.*
> Simbuman, 23
> – 13 years with a missionary organisation

The weight of representing a country, even in a small way, can be heavy. If you lived like this for most of your childhood, you may never have stopped to notice and acknowledge the weight of responsibility you felt. Even if you refused it, shirked it, wanted nothing to do with it, the shadow of that representation can haunt a person.

> **"**
> *I really felt it was important to put the good side of Australia forward when I was with others. But in many ways I did not represent Australia well as I did not know it well.*
> Brush, 70
> – 12 years with a missionary organisation

If, on the other hand, you were in a position to blend in, with a skin tone or accent that was unremarkable in your community, it may have rarely come up. One-quarter of our cohort said they sometimes or often hid their Australian-ness in order to fit in overseas, whether as children or adults.

Whatever the situation, whether you often represented Australia or were rarely noticed as Australian, it is common for Australian TCKs to feel disconnected from Australia at some point. To arrive in Australia and realise you don't fit in completely in the place you were always known for. Or to keep filling in 'Australia' on forms while knowing little about the country and feeling it had no impact on who you are.

"
Being Australian was one of the coolest defining features of my life/history/personality when I was outside Australia. Being from outside Australia was the biggest and most important thing about me when I was in Australia. I was constantly battling stereotypes and misconceptions wherever I was from both sides.
Wren, 20
– 18 years with a missionary organisation

"
Australia was a concept of which I had no personal experience. It was a map on the wall of 'home', which didn't feel true to the home I had.
Kimberley, 35
– 7 years with a missionary organisation

The reality is, connection to Australia *is* part of who you are. Wherever you are and wherever you go, this will be part of your story. It is not your whole story – there is more to you and your life – but it is *one* part of you. Learning more about Australia, its history and society and culture, can be helpful and sometimes healing. It can give you answers to the questions people pose, but more importantly, it can help you better understand the country stamped on that passport you carry.

Integrate your Australian heritage while overseas

1. Connect with Australians
Get to know some Australians, whether they live near you, or you connect virtually. Ask questions, learn things. Hear the Australian accent in real time. Have fun together! Let the sounds of that accent be associated with fun in your mind.

2. Connect through stories

Follow Australians on Instagram/TikTok/etc. who are telling their stories and sharing their lives. Ask Australians you connect with for stories. Learn about what their lives are/ were like. Let stories of 'ordinary life' in Australia seep into your sense of what is 'normal' through their stories. If you have cousins in Australia, they can be a great source of these kinds of stories. Take lots of time to listen, to learn what their normal is and what Australian life is like through their eyes.

3. Connect through media

In the digital age we have access to all sorts of media, no matter where we live. Take advantage of this to get to know some Australian media – be it TV shows, the media, music, books, or anything else you're interested in. Find things that *you* enjoy, rather than your exposure to Australian media being second-hand through your parents – and therefore probably a generation out of date!

4. Anzac Day services overseas

Anzac Day* is Australia's largest war commemoration observance. Dawn services are a big part of the tradition, and many Australian embassies around the world host dawn services which Australian citizens are welcome to attend (often co-hosted with the local New Zealand embassy). They are both unique and familiar everywhere, and are a great way to connect with Australian history and community wherever you are, especially if you live near an embassy. This was the one truly 'Australian' thing I (Tanya) did most years when I lived outside Australia as an adult.

5. Learn about Australia Day

January 26th is a national holiday for Australia Day* and often provides an 'excuse' for Australians abroad to celebrate their Australian-ness out loud, in communities where they are often in the minority. Many international communities pay attention to each other's national days, to recognise each country once a year. This day can feel special in international communities. At the same time, it is important to understand that Australia Day is more contentious within Australia –

there is a big movement to 'change the date' so it does not fall on 'Invasion Day' (anniversary of the day the continent was colonised, beginning two hundred years of massacres and other violent mistreatment of the Indigenous inhabitants). This can be painful for TCKs who have grown up celebrating Australia Day abroad without being taught the other side of the story. The answer is not to skip celebrating Australia, but to make sure you're learning a holistic history of our country.

Chapter 2:

Patriotism

Patriotism is a fraught subject for most Third Culture Kids. It is generally understood as a feeling of identity with and love for one country above all others. If you live overseas because a parent works for DFAT or the ADF, this can particularly strengthen the one-country-above-all idea of patriotism. Most TCKs, however, lack a comprehensive connection to a single country, so the idea that they can be patriotic at all is tricky.

66
I don't feel patriotic. I don't really understand patriotism that much. I've never really felt like I belong to a single country, and besides, countries are arbitrary lines drawn on maps by humans and they change over time. I love Australia – it's a beautiful country. But it's not the only beautiful country.
Shellie, 54
– 1 year with the ADF

66
I enjoy living in Australia, but tend to only feel patriotic towards Australia when I am outside the country!
Tamar, 50
– 18 years in the business sector

66
I don't think I've ever taken pride in being Malaysian or Australian. And the Cronulla riots* made me resent the Australian flag. But then I don't feel Malaysian either. If I could represent Malaysia in rugby that would be awesome, and if the Wallabies* play, I cheer for them!
Siew Ling, 38
– 16 years for family reasons

Is patriotism exclusive?

So, what is patriotism in a Third Culture context? While many people see patriotism as commitment to a single country, it doesn't have to be this way. It is possible to feel identity with and love for more than one country. Many TCKs feel connection to and affection for multiple countries. Giving yourself permission to see patriotism in a more expansive way can help you integrate these different aspects of your life experience.

> **"**
> *I love more than one country because multiple countries have contributed towards making me who I am.*
> Olivia, 23
> – 10 years with a missionary organisation

> **"**
> *I love more than one country because I have core memories in more than one country.*
> John, 28
> – 3 years with a missionary organisation

This is where the concept we call Inclusive Patriotism comes in handy. It means you can hold affection for and have commitment to more than one place at once. Maybe you will feel equally strongly about each place; maybe you will feel more strongly about one than another. Maybe your feelings will change over time. You might even find that over time you identify almost exclusively with a single country (even Australia). The country or countries you identify with and care about isn't what matters. What matters is accepting that this plurality is possible.

> **"**
> *I like having the mix in my life; I get uncomfortable when there's no mix. For the Olympics, I'm loyal to Papua New Guinea – I'll support PNG no matter who they're competing against. Then Australia, then America. During the last Olympics, I felt the need to instil this in my son a little bit (even though he was only six months old and had no concept of national identity) so I showed him the Michael Phelps races.*
> Jean, 33
> – 18 years with a missionary organisation

Inclusive Patriotism means that it is possible to love more than one place, and that it is not a betrayal of one place to care about another.

That is, you can be Australian and love or appreciate Australia, and *also* love and appreciate another country, or several other countries. To appreciate Australia is not a betrayal of another country that is also home to you. To love that other country is not being disloyal to Australia.

Inclusive Patriotism accepts that relationships are complicated – even relationships with countries. Feelings can grow, and wane, over time. Three-quarters of our cohort called Australia home – but two-thirds of those called more than one country home.

66
   Nepal always feels like home. But Australia feels like home, too. Mum and Dad did a lovely job of keeping up with our extended family so Australia always felt like a family place to come back to. But actually feeling at home took a while. Sometime in my teens or early twenties it started to feel like home, then I felt fine to say it's okay to have two homes – I'm not being disloyal to Nepal.
Georgia, 38
– 9 years with a missionary organisation

How others react to Inclusive Patriotism

While Inclusive Patriotism is a helpful concept and even a relief for many TCKs, not everyone sees patriotism this way. Many Australians experience exclusive patriotism to Australia. Indeed, many people worldwide experience exclusive patriotism to their passport countries. How do these people react to the Inclusive Patriotism of TCKs?

66
   I think because my family is from here I feel people disapprove if I don't call myself Australian. I've been here so long now that no other country has had a bigger time influence over me. But I don't want to say I'm Australian because I feel like that excludes all my other experiences.
Amy, 23
– 12 years with a missionary organisation

THONGS OR FLIP-FLOPS? 🩴

> **"**
> *Even though I'm Australian, I still have an affinity to the country where I grew up and the country where I lived as an adult. My friends and family find this difficult to understand at times.*
> David, 61
> – 6 years in aid and development

If your family see patriotism in an exclusive way, they may expect you to have exclusive love and loyalty for Australia above all other countries. If these family members hear you express stronger attachment to another country, or a lack of interest in or appreciation for Australia, they may feel you have rejected the country they love – the country they believe you should love too. This is true even for some who immigrated to Australia; having made sacrifices to bring their family to Australia, they struggle to understand why those family members would fail to appreciate it.

It is not your job to fix these misunderstandings. A strong dose of self-compassion and empathy for where they are coming from will help. Having caring friends or family who understand the situation and will listen to you is important for your own wellbeing. Sometimes it will be important to explain yourself; other times, you may choose to let things slide because an argument won't be worth your energy. Whatever choice you make in your own situation is completely fine.

> **"**
> *I identify as 100% Canadian and 100% Australian. Some people will say, 'Oh, so you're half Canadian and half Australian,' and I will fight them on that. No, I'm 100% both. Both have shaped me and influenced me. I have roots in both. If I denied one or the other, I'd be cutting off parts of myself.*
> Lyndall, 30
> – 5 years for family reasons

Pretending to be Australian

Having family members misunderstand your Inclusive Patriotism, especially when it does include Australia, can be frustrating and hurtful.

Patriotism

It hurts when a country you care about is dismissed. It hurts when your connection to your passport country is questioned.

You may feel you need to pretend for them, and hide who you really are. You may feel that they are rejecting a country or countries you care about – and rejecting that country feels like a rejection of you. Not seeing how much that country means to you means they don't understand you.

Friends and even strangers can also bring up these feelings. It's amazing how easy it is to say the 'wrong' thing and have people accuse you of not caring about Australia, caring more about another country than Australia, being a 'bad' Australian, or the classic, being 'un-Australian'.

Many Australian TCKs internalise these ideas – feeling like a 'bad' Australian when we do/don't do certain things. For example, I (Tanya) used to call myself a 'bad Australian' for not liking beer (though my tastes have changed, and I now enjoy the odd beer). Of course, there's nothing inherently 'Australian' about liking beer. It's an expression of feeling 'other' because of a trait I didn't share with many of my countrymates. Here are some other ways Aussie TCKs have internalised these feelings of difference:

> **66**
> *I feel like a 'bad Australian' when I say I don't want to live in Australia.*
> Milly, 21
> – 10 years for family reasons

> **66**
> *I feel like a 'bad Australian' when I don't recognise or appreciate iconic songs, places, shows, moments, etc. that others do.*
> Olivia, 23
> – 10 years with a missionary organisation

> **66**
> *I sometimes feel like a 'bad Australian' when I don't drink, don't subscribe to the 'Australian dream', and don't necessarily agree with the general consensus on a political topic.*
> Derek, 45
> – 10 years with a missionary organisation

> **"**
> *I feel like a 'bad Australian' when I admit I have zero interest in sport. I also struggle to remember the words to the national anthem!*
> Tamar, 50
> – 18 years in the business sector

> **"**
> *I feel 'un-Australian' when I don't fully support Australia in sports against countries I'm linked to, or don't fully support the actions of the country (for example, its racism).*
> David, 61
> – 6 years in aid and development

While there are hundreds of ways to be Australian, being 'other' often feels uncomfortable. You may feel the need to add an Australian mask on top of yourself, to make yourself more 'palatable' to the Australians you spend time with. This is a quick fix, a way to get through, but not something we recommend. It will hurt your relationship with Australia and Australians in the long run. And although people don't always understand you, there is nothing wrong with you. You might choose to accommodate them a bit, but you don't have to hide who you are.

> **"**
> *As a child wanting to fit in, I worked hard to change my accent, learn the slang, and find out what all the pop culture references were. This means that I now have an Australian facade, while I just kind of float in space and exist in this country with no real attachment. I hope to move away again soon and distance myself from the awfulness here.*
> Rosie, 25
> – 6 years with DFAT

Connecting with Australians

Connection matters. Faking a connection to Australia in order to feel connected can backfire, but there are other things we can do. Here are some alternative approaches you can try:

1. **Share what you care about**
   Tell people the things you do appreciate about Australia; let them see that while you might be connected to more than one place, you do see good things in the country they love.

2. **I'm still learning**
   If you spent a lot of time outside Australia, give yourself permission to tell people you are still a learner! Cultivate curiosity and learn more about this 'foreign' place stamped on the front of your passport.

3. **What can you teach me?**
   Ask people questions! Ask them to tell you what is great about Australia, or what they think you should know. This takes the focus off you and allows you to listen to them. You might learn something about Australia, but you'll definitely learn something about them. It's likely they'll share something you know and can agree with or affirm, which will help strengthen your relationship with them.

Rejecting Australia

While putting on an Australian mask is one way to respond to the hurt of being misunderstood, there are other ways to cope. Common reactions include withdrawing, or rejecting the people causing the hurt – and the place they represent: "if Australians can't accept me, I won't accept them!"

If you find yourself tempted down one of these avenues, don't worry – it's a completely normal and understandable reaction. Letting hurt control your choices is not healthy, however.

Mindset shifts

If you find yourself feeling extremely negative towards Australia, especially while in conversation with Australians, here are some prompts to help direct your thoughts outwards, in a way that is more likely to help you:

1. **There are millions of Australians**
    Australia is a diverse country. If you feel like 'the only one' in a conversation, a room, a school – remember that there are millions more Australians out there you haven't met yet. It's likely that many of them believe the same things you do, and see the same problems you do.

2. **Australia includes me**
    When you want to lash out at Australia/Australians, remember that you are included in that group – whether you want to be or not. Try using 'we/us' language when talking about Australia, rather than 'you/they' language. Remember how big the entirety of Australia is. It's big enough to include you, your discomforts, and your complaints. It is totally valid to struggle in your passport country – that doesn't mean you aren't part of Australia.

3. **I'm still learning**
    Australia is a big country, with millions of people who do not all share the same opinions. You won't convince everyone – but you can learn from them. Understanding where their different opinions come from can be enlightening, and the respect shown by listening to their story will usually earn you the right to tell your own story as well.

    "
    I think when I was younger and less accepting of being Australian, I criticised Australia for things I probably should have learned to cope with – like the adaptable TCK I am in other countries. That annoyed my extended family. Now, I accept my identity as Australian, so when I criticise Australia it's no longer as an outsider looking down. If I criticise Australians (which I do, frequently), I include myself, which I think makes it a lot more palatable to other Australians. Fair enough, too.
    Katie, 24
    – 14 years with a missionary organisation

Chapter 3:

Attending School Outside Australia

Being the Australian at school

Australians make up a small percentage of the world's population, so it's unsurprising that many Australian TCKs overseas find themselves the only Australian in their class – or even in their school. Some can blend into an international mix or have accents that blend with the American or British accents of their classmates. Others stand out – and know it.

> **"**
> *I was at an American school for the beginning of high school. I would spell 'favourite' and 'colour' the Australian way. I was determined to stand up for this, even if I lost half marks in English class. My teacher was Australian but the school followed the American curriculum. It was really important to me to keep this part of my life. I would also use the word 'toilet' instead of 'bathroom', although it was a bit impolite at that school.*
> Zoe, 35
> – 14 years with a missionary organisation

Some Australian TCKs like to stand out. To be Australian is to be different, and for some it comes with notoriety, or even popularity. Those who do not enjoy their host country may cling to an Australian identity – and the knowledge that they can call somewhere else 'home'. Unfortunately, the real Australia doesn't always live up to the hype.

Even those who prefer to stay under the radar, or who don't feel particularly Australian, often find themselves roped into representing Australia at school events. Most international schools and even many local schools enjoy celebrating the diversity of their student body. Whether it's for an international day, global festival, or something else, students are encouraged to do things such as wear their 'national dress', bring their 'local food' in for others to try, or carry their national flag in a parade.

> **"**
> *For days like Australia Day, the Australian students might dress up with Aussie flags and wear the green-and-gold*. My international friends did like Anzac Day* because the Aussies in my community taught them to make Anzac biscuits*, and everyone liked them. One American teacher made my class Anzac biscuits for Anzac Day, and I felt very touched and included.*
> Alex, 23
> – 13 years with a missionary organisation

Wearing 'national dress' can be a bit tricky for Australians. How exactly do we do that? Wear a sports uniform? Dress up as a bushranger* or perhaps Steve Irwin*? There's no easy answer. And many costume ideas ignore the history of Indigenous Australians, which is also very difficult to represent in a responsible way if you are not of Aboriginal ancestry.

Our offerings for 'national food' might include lamingtons*, fairy bread*, Vegemite*, and damper*. Indigenous ingredients are becoming more popular within Australia but are almost impossible to find outside the country. That said, some indigenous spices can be brought from Australia and kept long term. Macadamia nuts are a great idea – a flexible native Australian crop that is recognised in much of the world. Or you can make pavlova* and argue over it with the Kiwis* – if you have access to an oven where you live!

Here are some ways Australian TCKs have celebrated these sorts of events:

> **"**
> *I felt like I was representing Australia when I held the flag at an assembly at the international school parade. On international days, we represented Australia with Vegemite*, fairy bread*, cricket*, and AFL*.*
> Olivia, 23
> – 10 years with a missionary organisation

"
We represented Australia by wearing our Akubras*, bringing ANZAC biscuits* or barbecue food, and wearing the Australian flag as a cape.
Simbuman, 23
– 13 years with a missionary organisation

"
We were one of the few Australian families at the school, so we were always the ones to represent Australia during the annual International Week. We wore very stereotypical Aussie things, like Akubras* with corks. One year I modelled a Sydney Olympics jacket on the 'runway'.
Sera, 34
– 15 years with a missionary organisation

"
We desperately avoided cringeworthy swagman* outfits by dressing in clothes representing our family's cultural heritage (Scottish/English) instead! Food-wise, we might take meat pies and tomato sauce or maybe damper* with golden syrup*.
Jane, 48
– 5 years in aid and development

Sometimes these sorts of events can make it hard for Australian TCKs to connect with our country, our family heritage, and our history as a colonised land and immigrant nation. Acknowledging this – by acknowledging your family's mixed cultural heritage, for example – can lead to good conversations.

School culture

Culture is something we learn in a community. Attending a school that has a different culture – whether local or international – means spending a lot of time learning cultural norms that will not apply in Australia. Classroom etiquette and the expectations of students change from school to school. Asking the teacher questions might get you into trouble. Or it might be a required part of your assessment. How do you know which one it is when you're launched into a new classroom? How do you even know what to ask?

Educational culture includes fundamental assumptions about the purpose of education. Australia's educational philosophy reflects the country's individualist values. As Jane Barron – educator and youth intercultural transition specialist at Globally Grounded – explains, "The Australian curriculum has been designed to educate the whole child through intellectual, physical, emotional, social, spiritual, and moral development. For students who have previously learned in an education system which focuses on academic development, this is a huge shift."

> **"**
> *When we started school in Australia in Year 11, we got involved with everything because it felt like a privilege – there's so many different opportunities, like sport and drama, and you could pick your subjects. You weren't told what to study. I think we recognised the privilege because we had come from a different setting and we appreciated it.*
> Siew Ling, 38
> – 16 years for family reasons

It is not just the purpose of education that changes from place to place; the method of instruction may look very different too. Australia not only uses a learner-centred educational style, but teachers also take a quite relaxed approach in the classroom. Jane Barron explains: "A student who has previously learned through a teacher-centred approach often finds the 'freedom' of the Australian education culture confusing and challenging. Australian teacher-student relationships tend to be more relational, relaxed, and analogous, where teachers are regarded as partners in learning. In contrast, education systems founded on the Confucius Discourse experience teacher-student relationships which are often more hierarchical, formal, and distant, where teachers are regularly regarded as superior to parents. For a student educated in this type of culture, imagine the shock of entering an Australian classroom where students are sitting in groups, sharing their perspectives with one another, and being asked to critically evaluate the learning of their peers as they work together towards a common goal, all while the teacher is walking around the classroom listening."

On the other hand, imagine the shock of the Australian TCK walking into a classroom in which they are expected to be quiet throughout class, call their teacher "sir", "ma'am", "teacher" or another title, and where educational success lies in memorising rather than critically examining the material presented.

It was common in my (Tanya's) final two years of high school for students to call our teachers by their given names – no title or surname at all. Group work (causing noisy classrooms) was common throughout my Australian school years. In contrast, other countries I studied in required lots of silent listening to a teacher, respectful titles for teachers all through high school and university, copying down lots of notes, or spending class time quietly copying out exercises.

Some Australian TCKs find the adjustment to an Australian school quite difficult, as they adjust to different expectations – both their own expectations of teachers and classmates, and the classmates' and teachers' expectations of them.

"
My classmates in Australia always felt so slack, rowdy, and disrespectful compared to my classmates overseas. I also felt incredibly bad whenever my Australian classmates would be rude, or disrespectful to the teachers. It just felt wrong for kids to be disrespectful to their elders.
Simbuman, 23
– 13 years with a missionary organisation

"
The Australian public school system was very relaxed compared to the US/Korean-based school I attended overseas and my peers there.
John, 28
– 3 years with a missionary organisation

For those who move at an older age, all the rules they learned for how to succeed in school may turn out to be not quite right, or even completely useless, in their new school – whether in Australia or overseas. The older you are, the more adults expect you to know what to do without being told. While a first grader's cultural error might be laughingly corrected, a teenager may be reprimanded – with the assumption that they did it on purpose.

❝

At school in Australia I didn't understand the rules or fit in. No one told me that my school socks were meant to be white; they just teased me instead.

Annabelle, 46

– 11 years with a missionary organisation

Whether you move from an Australian classroom to a classroom in another country, repatriate to an Australian classroom, or both, these transitions can be stressful. It takes time to learn the rules and work out what it takes to be a successful student in a new school environment. As we will discuss later, however, returning to your passport country can be a trickier move because of the expectation that you 'should' fit in and know the rules.

International schools

When a school is called an 'international' school, it usually means the curriculum (and perhaps language of instruction) is different to the norms of the national curriculum where the school is located. Even when the student body and teaching staff are a true mix of nationalities, the curriculum used will have a big impact on what is taught, and how it is taught. The vast majority of Australian TCKs attending international schools are not attending schools using the Australian curriculum, and the school environment is not at all Australian. TCKs attending local schools outside Australia are definitely not in an Australian school environment.

❝

We attended a very international school – 300 students from kindergarten to 12th grade, from 78 countries. There were a lot of Japanese returnees – Japanese kids who went overseas for a couple of years but then returned to Japan and couldn't fit back into Japanese school – and then there was us: a mishmash of international kids that came from all over the world, all ethnicities and religions. It was an amazing experience. I think all of us felt very special and privileged to have grown up in such a truly international community."

Lisa, 45

– 17 years in the business sector

Australian TCKs often don't receive lessons in Australian history and geography. We do not learn about our land and our history while attending schools that have different curriculums based on the history and geography of other countries. Many Australian TCKs who have never lived in the USA know more about its history and geography than they do of Australia's – because of the curriculum of the schools they attended overseas.

> **"**
> *I found that I knew very little about Australian history compared to my peers.*
> Simbuman, 23
> – 13 years with a missionary organisation

> **"**
> *A lot of the grammar, spelling, history, and geography taught by the American curriculum was very different to the Australian curriculum. I didn't learn about geography outside of the United States or Europe until returning to Australia. Most students were American, so this made sense when they returned to schooling in the US. For me, this made it tricky when I returned to Australia with different knowledge to my fellow students.*
> Rebecca, 33
> – 5 years with a missionary organisation

Changing curriculums

Another difficult experience many Australian TCKs face is changing curriculums. To begin with, while Australia generally uses the terms 'Year 8' and 'Grade 8' interchangeably, these mean different things in other curriculums. 'High school' in Australia usually means Grades 7–10, and sometimes includes Grades 11–12. In the US system, high school usually means Grades 9–12. In British curriculum international schools, the term 'Year' is used, but their Year 7 is equivalent to US Grade 6. On top of this, some parts of Australia (most notably the ACT) call Grades 11–12 'college'. And every state is a little different, especially the name for kindergarten (prep/transition) in each location.

Curriculums around the world have different approaches to teaching subjects such as literature, mathematics, science, history, and geography.

Even the basics of spelling and handwriting can be very different from one curriculum to another. Jane Barron explains: "Curriculum is a crucial factor in student academic success. Some curriculums are content-rich, others are skills-based and others, like Australia's National Curriculum, are a combination of the two. When a student changes curriculum, there will inevitably be gaps in both their knowledge and their skills. Curriculum generally builds upon what has previously been learned, year-on-year. What is valued in one curriculum may be entirely different from what is valued in another curriculum." Seven of the ten cohort members who repatriated to Australia before the age of 18 found the change in curriculum difficult.

> **"**
> *When I changed curriculums, I had to relearn things like maths notation and science vocabulary, and I didn't know how to write an essay.*
> Amelie, 18
> – 10 years with a missionary organisation

> **"**
> *The US system for maths was incredibly siloed by giving us a year of each topic, whereas Australia goes through a small portion of each topic each year and has separate tiers for students with differing abilities.*
> Simbuman, 23
> – 13 years with a missionary organisation

> **"**
> *Each school taught different mathematics concepts at different times. As a result, I was always catching up on something and ended up in second level maths subjects, which affected my university pathway.*
> Derek, 45
> – 10 years with a missionary organisation

One of the difficulties in changing curriculums is that it can be very difficult to assess where a student is 'up to'. It is possible to be at different grade levels in different subjects. A student may be repeating content in one class while being 'in over their head' in another. Whatever the situation, and no matter how much support is given, this is stressful.

On top of this, the Australian school year runs from January to December, whereas northern hemisphere schools (and curriculums) use a different school year, often beginning in August or September and ending around June. For Australian TCKs, this divergence in school years can create all sorts of hurdles when it comes to moving countries.

Jane Barron explains: "The most vexing question for families who change hemispheres is 'which grade should my child go in to?' Should they go up or down a grade? Changing hemispheres often means students arrive or leave part way through the academic year, which can impact them socially, emotionally, and academically. As a leaver, being unable to finish the year alongside friends can add to the grief of saying goodbye. As an arriver, the official school orientation program often does not cater for those who arrive 'out-of-synch' and may leave new students feeling invisible. As humans, our emotions support our cognition so when it comes to changing hemispheres, prioritising the social and emotional wellbeing of a child will support their academic development."

"
I went to an international school that ran on the northern hemisphere school year. Whenever I came back to Australia it was difficult to figure out which year level I would fit into. I was in Year 1 for eighteen months and did six months of Year 6. By the time I got to high school, my parents decided it would be easier for me to stick with the northern hemisphere school system. This meant that I would sometimes stay overseas to go to school while my family went to Australia for a few months. This was difficult for me, but it meant that I got to finish school with minimal interruptions.
Alex, 23
– 13 years with a missionary organisation

"
Initially I had to go into a special class to get up to speed with the American system; I really struggled with that. Then they changed to content I'd already learned back in Australia, so I went from the bottom of the class straight to the top of the class. I stepped back half a year to get in line with the American system and then I had to step back another half a year to get back in line with the Australians.
Dave, 35
– 4 years with a missionary organisation

66

I ended up going to three schools in the year we moved from Sydney to New Jersey. Looking back, I don't know why my parents didn't wait a month or two to arrive in the US during the summer holidays. They never considered the effects of all these transitions and brief stints. They just thought kids adapt.
Christina, 59
– 13 years in the business sector

In my case (Tanya), I completed Grade 8 and the first term of Grade 9 in Australia. Then I moved to the US where I did the final quarter of Grade 8, all of Grade 9, and half of Grade 10. Two weeks later I was in Australia beginning Grade 11. With the curriculum differences, I ended up 18 months behind my Australian peers in mathematics and missed out on large portions of the social studies curriculum, as well as rites of passage such as work experience*, the Year 10 Formal* and high school (Grade 10) graduation.

66

I left Australia halfway through the school year. I had a far more restricted choice of subjects in the US and had to drop geography, German, and music, but added a science subject. Back in Australia, I was able to finish Year 10 at my old high school in the ACT so I'd at least have my Year 10 certificate from there. However, the following year we moved to QLD and yet another school system. The ACT and QLD might as well have been two different hemispheres in terms of curriculum. I found it very difficult to settle – three school systems in two countries in 18 months was too much.
Shellie, 54
– 1 year with the ADF

Jane Barron concludes: "Whilst every child and situation is unique, as a 30-year veteran in the field of education, I am yet to meet a parent who has regretted prioritising social and emotional wellbeing by holding their child back. I have, however, met countless parents who have regretted prioritising academic development by sending them up a grade. Students who are encouraged and supported to make and build social connections, and who are equipped with knowledge and understanding to effectively address the triumphs and trials of crossing cultures and hemispheres are more likely to thrive in all aspects of their new school."

Entering Australian universities

In addition to this, the final two years of high school in Australia are often geared towards university entrance. Coming in during this period can be rough, and trying to enter Australian universities as a local citizen without attending an Australian high school can be even tougher! Australia has improved the system in recent years, however. The IB Diploma and Bilingual Diploma are recognised as equivalent to an Australian Year 12 qualification.

In addition, senior secondary studies (Grades 11 and 12) undertaken in English-speaking countries, at a difficulty level comparable with the NSW HSC (Higher School Certificate), are recognised as 'assessable qualifications'. This means you can submit your qualification to UAC (the Universities Admissions Centre), who will assess it and give you a corresponding ATAR (Australian Tertiary Admission Rank) based on it.

These qualifications can be submitted to UAC for a Qualifications Assessment Service (QAS) before applying for university admission to see how your qualifications are likely to rank; the fee for this service was $140 as of 2023. This is an optional service to help you plan before officially applying to UAC as a student. (More information can be found at the UAC website: uac.edu.au.)

> **"**
> *For university enrolment, I applied as a domestic, citizen, and student with international qualifications, which were incredibly difficult to explain, and I had to call up UAC and my potential universities to explain my situation – which none of them understood – and it took over a month for my application to be approved for review.*
> Mei Mei, 22
> – 10 years with a missionary organisation

> *I gained an ATAR through an American high school diploma. The way the Australian system translates American results into an ATAR has fluctuated over time so it's a bit stressful because the process is not explained well. My academic strengths and results translated very well and were viewed very optimistically. I was given a 99.95, even though I was not as well rounded a student as those who were awarded that score through the HSC. They may have wised up to that sort of loophole now.*
Tom, 27
– 18 years with a missionary organisation

Jane Barron offers this sage advice: "For Australian citizen students who have completed their secondary education abroad, returning to Australia for tertiary studies can be a complex transition. They may look and sound just like their fellow students who have been educated in neighbourhood schools near their new university, but their life and educational experiences are entirely different. Studying at university is a time of exploration. Embracing the university environment which fosters curiosity can lead students towards discovering their authentic selves."

> *Being overseas meant a loss of appreciation for career choices available in Australia when I did return, and many lost years unsure what my future should be. For example, there was no appreciation for working in the trades.*
Jesse, 38
– 3 years with a missionary organisation

Most TCKs make do with whatever situation we find ourselves in. We find a way forward and keep on keeping on. This adaptable attitude does not remove the stress of these situations, especially if we feel unseen or unsupported at the time (whether or not this is objectively true).

> *I had to go back six months as I moved overseas halfway through Grade 10. Then when we moved back, I had to wait six months for university enrolment in January. So really I ended up a year behind. The life experience was worth it though.*
John, 28
– 3 years with a missionary organisation

Practising self-compassion

Often, the stresses of school interruptions are underestimated, whether by others or by ourselves. We may have negative self-talk about struggles we've had and that we have perceived as 'failures'. When this is the case, self-compassion can be a powerful tool. Dr Rachel Cason, TCK counsellor and author of *Incredible Lives and the Courage to Live Them*, explains that self-compassion is not a way to deny reality, but "facing the reality you are experiencing, and instead of dismissing this reality as less than it is, really seeing it and its impact on you". Having done this, she continues, we can "choose to relate to ourselves with compassion" and in so doing, "become our own safe space, a place we can come to for comfort and love. Not as a cocoon from reality, but to ground ourselves firmly in it, in ourselves and make sure we remain firmly on our own side."

If you have dealt with curriculum changes, hemisphere changes, messed up school years, changes in school culture, or anything of that nature, try taking a moment to reflect on those transitions. Think about how it felt as a child or teenager in that position. Notice any stress you feel in your body when you think back to that situation. Take a few deep breaths. Now speak words of encouragement to the child/teen you were at the time. Give yourself the compassion you did not receive – or give yourself – at the time. What would you say? If you aren't sure, try some of these:

- You are doing a great job in a stressful situation.
- You have done nothing wrong.
- Taking extra time to complete school doesn't mean you are a bad student.
- No one has explained the rules to you, but you will work them out as you go.
- I know this feels overwhelming, and that's okay.
- It's not your fault that this is hard.
- Relax, you've got this. You'll get the hang of it with a little time.

Chapter 4:

Language

Speaking 'Australian'

English is the common language of Australia, but Australians have a unique way of speaking English – with their own slang and vocabulary, accent, and style.

> **"**
> *I've learned that even in countries where English is the national language, my 'English' is very different and can be hard to understand to those who haven't had much cross-cultural exposure. Even in a shared language, my 'otherness' is apparent.*
> Kimberley, 35
> – 7 years with a missionary organisation

> **"**
> *I found that Australian speech sounded very slurred since we speak fast. Our accent is not what makes our words confusing; it's the fast pace at which we spit them out that loses our listeners.*
> Tayo, 21
> – 6 years with the ADF

TCKs growing up overseas can be surprised by how differently Australians speak in Australia compared to how the Australian expatriates they knew abroad spoke. Australian TCKs may think they sound Australian themselves, until they repatriate. 60% of those in our cohort who repatriated to Australia as children struggled with their changed accent. I (Tanya) was only gone for two years as a teenager and had zero idea my accent had shifted away from a 'standard' Australian accent until after I repatriated.

> **"**
> *When I returned I had an American accent. I hadn't realised I had it till I came home and went to school.*
> Fayette, 61
> – 1 year with the education sector

Dr Michael Carey, Senior Lecturer in English Language and Literacy at the School of Education in QLD, explains that, "The main defining feature of an accent is the vowel quality. English has a complex vowel space, with about 20 vowel sounds in Australian English. The vowel space of an international school accent will match the English language, without specifically matching any particular regional accent."

> **"**
> *I had a British/international accent when I repatriated to Australia as a child, and had difficulty understanding Aussie slang. My accent became Australian quite quickly, but I didn't purposefully do this – it just happened. Though I still say some words differently.*
> Josie, 35
> – 7 years with a missionary organisation

There are some variations in Australian accents, but research shows that this is less about region and more about social class; the different Australian accents are defined as 'sociolects' as they are identified by social strata. Dr Carey explains: "There are three categories of Australian accent long defined as: broad, general, and cultivated. There is sociolectical variation, but no regional variation. Wealth, education, and social strata are not always tightly connected. Broad doesn't always mean regional, or lower class, or poor, or uneducated. Movement from city to country and vice versa has further muddied any regional accent zones that may have existed previously. Sociolectical accent difference in Australia, even though we aren't class conscious, says something about that person. It might not say 'I'm working class', but it might say 'I'm more Australian than you' or 'I'm more educated than you'."

> **"**
> *I vary even within my Australian accent. My most natural accent (which I use in Sydney and which sounds a bit British) becomes much more 'ocker*' when visiting my parents on the South Coast or speaking with people who use a broad Australian accent.*
> Toby, 30
> – 15 years with a missionary organisation

Accent changes

Everyone has an accent, in every language they speak. An accent is the combination of the differences in how we pronounce all the sounds of a language. We learn how to make sounds by listening to the people we are around, and mimicking how they pronounce things. We do this automatically as young children, not knowing what we are doing as we do it. Intercultural Language and Communication Consultant Dr Ute Limacher-Riebold explains: "Developing children typically acquire languages by imitating sounds and intonations from people around them. From very early on they make attempts to imitate sounds, then sound-chains, from monosyllables to more complex words to sentences and so on."

Some of us continue to do this as we grow older, unconsciously mimicking the accents of those we spend time around. Dr Carey explains that this gets complicated when "TCKs are receiving a mixture of phonologies while they are developing their own phonology [understanding of how sounds relate to each other]. The dominant exposure will usually be what they pick up." Some of us maintain a single accent, but it might change over time, sliding towards the pronunciations we hear most commonly around us. Some of us develop a few different accents we switch between – this is colloquially called 'code-switching', though as Dr Carey explains, "Code-switching is usually used for language; phonological adaptation is the phrase for accent code-switching."

66

I don't have an Australian accent, but I use the Australian pronunciation of certain words. If I first learned a word in the Australian accent (e.g. no worries, reckon*, bugger*, Queenslanda*), I might say it with Australian flair.
Darren, 38
– 17 years in the education sector

Dr Limacher-Riebold says, "Code-switching happens for several reasons. For example, the desire to fit in or adapt to a particular group or social context, to connect with a group or to show solidarity with a community, or to reinforce their identity. Multilinguals switch accents depending on the languages they are speaking in order to signal their identity or belonging to a particular linguistic community. Code-switching our accent is very natural in multilingual and multicultural contexts. We can switch between different accents and languages to better communicate with those who may not share our linguistic background. Accent code-switching can have many different functions and can be influenced by several factors like social context, identity and linguistic ability."

> **"**
> *People in Australia are often surprised I didn't lose my Australian accent – even though I mostly spoke English at home with my parents. Although I also learned to speak English with a Spanish accent so my peers in Spain could actually understand me. I often subconsciously change the way I speak to match who I'm speaking to. For example, I worked at a café run by a Lebanese couple and, while I used an Australian accent with customers, found myself mirroring my employers' accents when I spoke with them!*
> Amelie, 18
> – 10 years with a missionary organisation

> **"**
> *I still code-switch accents at nearly 50! I'm always worried people will think I'm trying to make fun of them, when I'm just doing it without being conscious of it!*
> Bron, 50
> – 5 years with a missionary organisation

Only a third of our cohort spoke purely in Australian accents. Another third had mixed accents that were mostly or somewhat Australian. One-quarter of them code-switched, with one of their accents being Australian, and 7% did not sound Australian at all.

> **"**
> *My accent, though Australian, is not too strong. I believe years living abroad makes me more like a chameleon with my accent, and my accent can fit the surroundings a bit more than the average Aussie.*
> Annabelle, 46
> – 11 years with a missionary organisation

Those in our cohort with an Australian accent said it was perceived by non-Australians as: interesting (39%), funny (33%), cute (25%), hard to understand/confusing (24%), exotic (22%), and laidback (20%). Those without an Australian accent said Australians described it as: interesting (32%), weird (28%), and funny (18%). Our cohort thought Australian accents sound: laidback (49%), normal (48%), friendly (34%), and comforting (19%).

Dr Limacher-Riebold says, "Accents and languages connect us to places." An accent places a person in geography, telling the world where they are 'from' – or at least, where their sounds are from. Because of this, many people have strong emotional reactions to accents – their own and others'. Australian TCKs with a strong attachment to their Australian identity can be distraught to learn that their accent does not sound Australian to others, or that it has changed over time and no longer sounds Australian.

"

I tell people I'm Australian, but I sound Canadian at first if they aren't listening closely. So then I'll tell my story and they say 'Oh, I didn't know you're Australian, you don't have an accent anymore.'
Lyndall, 30
– 5 years for family reasons

Australian TCKs who do not have an Australian accent may find their Australian identity is questioned by others, both Australians and internationals. Some even feel pressure to sound more Australian – including nearly half of our cohort! 28% of our cohort experienced this pressure from Australian peers, and 14% from non-Australian peers. This can be distressing for some (17% of our cohort put pressure on themselves to sound more Australian!) though others enjoy the anonymity of being mistaken for Americans, Brits, or other nationalities.

"

As a child, I lived in the international community, where I was more easily accepted as an Australian by other TCKs experiencing their own form of cultural dysmorphia. But residing in the United States, it feels like a lie when I say that I am Australian. People don't understand how or why I am Australian when I don't have an Australian accent.
Darren, 38
– 17 years in the education sector

66

People inside and outside of Australia assume I'm not Australian because of my accent and how I present. But I am, and whenever I go overseas, I know it all over again.
Chris, 58
– 1 year in the business sector

Dr Limacher-Riebold says, "The way we speak reveals a lot about where we come from, where we have lived. Hearing someone with a particular accent can evoke images and feelings associated with that place. Hearing particular accents or languages can create a sense of belonging and identity. When we hear someone who speaks one of our languages or when we recognize a familiar accent, we can feel a sense of connection and community. The same also works in the opposite direction: if someone speaks one of our languages with a different accent than we expect, we can feel a sense of separation, even tension or rejection. In my opinion, languages and accents are very important for maintaining cultural heritage, as many accents are tied to a specific region or community. Maintaining them – also when living abroad – can help us consolidate our very unique cultural identity that connects us to those places."

66

The Australian accent brings out a dichotomy in me! On one hand, the Australian accent undeniably sounds like home to me. Particularly overseas, it is comforting and familiar and warm. But I also think it sounds unsophisticated ('bogan'!) and have always actively resisted the broadest Australian sounds in my own accent. It's only in the last few years that I have been more accepting of my Australian accent.*
Matthew, 35
– 9 years with a missionary organisation

Having an accent that is not quite – or not at all – Australian can also be difficult for an Australian TCK's parents. Some parents feel stressed or guilty about it, worrying that their kids will not fit in when they go 'home' to Australia. They may force their kids to speak a certain way, or correct their pronunciation, in an attempt to make them sound 'more Australian'. 16% of our cohort experienced pressure from parents or extended family to make their accent more Australian. This can be confusing or stressful for a child who cannot find a linguistic refuge anywhere – not even in their own home.

Dr Carey explains that phonological adaptation (code-switching accents) is a normal neurological process – something that may comfort many TCKs and their parents: "The speech perception and speech production areas of our brains are activated simultaneously when we are listening and speaking. When we listen to someone speak, the area of our brain that produces speech is paying attention. This is why we drift into this other way of speaking – because our ears are telling us to. And we will drift back again. Not because we decide to, not because we go to a teacher or speech pathologist, but because it's a natural process. It happens faster for some than others, that's just natural and idiosyncratic."

66

I grew up in an international community with a lot of Americans. When I first came back to Australia at age six, I had a strong American twang to my accent. Some people thought I wasn't my Australian parents' kid! As I grew up, my dad encouraged me to keep my Aussie accent. I would watch Aussie movies and be conscious of how my accent sounded. Now as an adult, I would describe my accent as 'ocker*' and stronger than my parents' accents because I worked so hard to not lose it.
Alex, 23
– 13 years with a missionary organisation

Australian reactions to an international accent

Having an international accent might be completely normal in an international school, and unremarkable outside Australia, but when in Australia it is a different story. Extended family members who have lived in Australia their whole lives may make unhelpful comments to Australian TCKs about their non-standard accents. Teasing a TCK about their accent, even when meant as 'just a joke', can be painful. Too often the message sent is that 'you don't belong here' whether or not it is the intent.

> **"**
> *Because I'd tried so hard to fit in, I lost my Aussie accent so that made it harder to claim Australian-ness later. I felt embarrassed when meeting Australians because I didn't sound Australian, and as time went on, I knew less and less about the evolving culture.*
> Christina, 59
> – 13 years in the business sector

In some Australian communities, being marked out as an international traveller is a negative – the assumption being that you must think you are better than others if you have travelled extensively (and they have not). This connects to a common theme in Australian culture: avoiding the appearance of arrogance (we'll talk more about this in *Chapter 7*). Talking about international life – and particularly sounding 'less Australian' – is sometimes perceived by Australians as arrogance.

When a non-standard accent is associated with migration to Australia, racism can be a problem. When a non-standard accent is associated with travel away from Australia, ascribed arrogance can be a problem. I (Tanya) encountered this negative prejudice as a 15-year-old meeting peers in Australia.

I (Kath) recently met a young adult Australian TCK with a thick European accent; she hated this during the first few years of her repatriation as people regularly made fun of her. After a while she decided to embrace her accent, however, and to love the story her voice carries.

American accents in particular tend to attract criticism in Australia. There is anti-American sentiment in many areas of Australian society. This is also often associated with the Australian horror of arrogance. Australians who will welcome individual Americans very warmly may yet give the cold shoulder to an Australian TCK with an American-influenced accent.

> **"**
> *I never lived in Australia, and the communities and teachers with whom I interacted were predominantly North American, so I developed an American accent rather than an Australian one. This led me to be explicitly ostracised by my Australian peers,*

and persistently othered by them. I constantly had to prove my Australian-ness by translating Australian slang, and would have to explain my Australian-ness to fellow Australians, much to their confusion and unacceptance. This still happens to this day. We were raised to be culturally Australian, with observing Australian holidays, watching Australian sport, and raised on Australiana. But I have never felt accepted by Australia, expatriate Australians, and domestic Australians.
Darren, 38
– 17 years in the education sector

Dr Carey has helpful advice to offer here: "It's about them, not you. Communication is a two-way street. The listener has a role as well. They have to be willing to participate in the conversation. Some people who aren't accustomed to perceptual adaptation will shut down." When this happens, the problem is their inability to adjust and adapt. The sound of your voice, whatever accent(s) you use, is never a problem – and there will be people who accept you as you are.

Making peace with your accent

1. **Trace the story of your accent**
    What has impacted your accent? What people, and places, have contributed to the unique way you speak each of your languages? When has your accent been accepted, or rejected? When has your way of speaking stood out, or fitted in?

2. **Investigate the emotions**
    Take time and create space to feel any emotions that this journey brings up for you. Do you have positive/negative emotions towards certain people/places that figure in your accent journey, due to these emotional connections?

3. **Take ownership of your accent**
    The TCK journey is often marked by many changes that are outside your control as a child. As you move into adulthood, you will start having more control over where you spend your time – and among which accents. The choice of where you live will impact your accent, one way or another. You

can also make choices about the media you consume and the people you connect with, in order to learn or maintain certain accents. Take ownership of these choices and how they change your accent over time as you move forward.

4. **Talk to someone**

    If you struggle with your accent, if you feel pressured to sound (or not sound) a certain way, talk to someone you feel emotionally safe with about your feelings. Perhaps this will be a parent, sibling, or friend. Perhaps it will be a coach or therapist with experience in the TCK world. You are not the only one who has been through this journey, and there are people who can help you.

Additional languages

Many TCKs (though not all) learn additional languages. These are languages in addition to English and any heritage languages the family speaks. For those TCKs who learn additional languages from a country (or more than one country) they have lived in, there are a few things worth noting.

Australia can be a difficult place to come to if you have been living in a place where multilingualism is the norm. In many parts of the world it is very common for people to speak two, three or more languages. In Australia, many people speak only English. Additional languages are usually heritage languages, spoken mostly at home with family. If you speak a little of an additional language, you may find Australians praising you for your language prowess – something that can feel very uncomfortable when you know just how much more linguistically competent others are.

One impact of Australia's lack of linguistic diversity is that it may be difficult to keep up your language ability – especially if you live outside the few big cities. Some languages can be accessed virtually through online media or learning apps like Duolingo, Memrise, or Babbel – but only those languages that are common/popular enough to get significant exposure.

> **"**
> *I'm definitely losing my Khmer, although it comes back when I visit Cambodia. I'm sad to lose it. You can't practise it on Duolingo, and it's not easy to access Khmer media, especially since I never learnt to read and write in Khmer. There are very few Khmer speakers in rural Australia – I've only met one other than my immediate family, a third-generation Khmer immigrant who only spoke a few words of Khmer. Occasionally on a visit to the city I can go to the suburbs where there are Khmer speakers but there's nothing like the language immersion I had in Cambodia. I love Khmer, and it's a part of me I can rarely bring out in Australia. I can talk about my experiences of culture and make the food, but language is hard to share. The only Khmer word I got friends using is for the taste and mouthfeel of unripe banana.*
> Katie, 24
> – 14 years with a missionary organisation

Most people will naturally lose some language competency with disuse. If you find yourself forgetting a language which was important to you, that you used to speak daily or were even fluent in, this can be devastating. As we have said, language connects us to place – and that includes places we have left, places we miss.

While there are practical things you can do to use your language, and you may enjoy that, it still won't be the same as when speaking it was part of your regular life. It can be therapeutic to create space to mourn that loss – to remember what it was like to speak the language regularly, and be sad that this is no longer your reality.

> **"**
> *I had a second fluent language as a child, but I 'lost' it within a year of coming back and stopping using it. I say 'lost' because I can't understand it anymore, but it isn't really lost, I still know it. It is familiar to me, but no longer holds meaning because in my brain it is not linked to English at all, so I can't associate any meaning to it.*
> Kelly, 37
> – 2 years with a missionary organisation

Learning language and accent

1. **Conversation with native speakers**

   One of the best ways to pick up a language or accent is to hear it in conversation. Talking with native speakers, hearing the way they talk to each other and being part of the conversation, is one of the best ways to adopt their speech patterns. As Dr Carey says: "Watching a few Australian movies isn't enough to adapt the Australian accent – interaction is important."

2. **Listen to media**

   There are lots of other ways to listen to a language or accent you connect with! You can watch TV shows or movies, and listen to podcasts or audiobooks. The more 'niche' your target language or accent is, the harder it will be to find media – but in our growing digital world there may be more than you realise. There are even lots of language-learning podcasts out there – perfect if you don't read the accompanying script! Watching soap operas is particularly helpful for language learning through media, as there is usually a lot of repeated content to help you revise vocabulary. Subtitled media can be good for language learning, but also a way to include friends in the culture you care about. I (Tanya) used to watch the show 非诚勿扰 (*If You Are the One*) with Australian friends after repatriating; they liked the show, and loved getting extra nuggets of insight from me related to Chinese language and culture.

3. **Linguistics**

   Learning about linguistics, and particularly phonetics (how sounds are produced) helps a lot when it comes to both language and accent learning. Accents exist because languages produce similar sounds slightly differently – placing the tongue in a slightly different place in the mouth to make a 't' or 'd' sound, for example. I (Tanya) find the podcast *Lingthusiasm* a great place to engage with, and point of entry to, linguistics.

Section 2:
When You 'Return' to Australia

Chapter 5:

Repatriation

Repatriation means moving to live in your passport country after living elsewhere for an extended period. It is the opposite of expatriation. The 'pat' part of these words comes from the Latin *patria* meaning country (fatherland). The prefix 'ex' means out of, and the prefix 're' means back or again. So an expatriate is a person living outside their passport country (perhaps for quite a long time) while a repatriate is a person returning to live in their passport country. The COVID-19 pandemic led to the single largest repatriation of Australian citizens in history. In the year ending June 2020, nearly 100,000 Australians repatriated (this and more information can be found at the Australian Bureau of Statistics: abs.gov.au).

Some repatriating TCKs are truly returning, while others are actually beginning their first experience of living in their passport country. Three-quarters of our cohort experienced repatriation to Australia as children; all but two of these shared struggles they had with the experience. Half the group experienced a single childhood repatriation, a quarter repatriated twice during childhood, and the rest repatriated three or more times before the age of 18.

In some ways, repatriation is just like any international move. The logistics of moving are similar, though a visa is not required. Some of the associated struggles could be part of any big move. 72% of our childhood repatriation cohort missed their friends, and 38% couldn't get the food they were used to.

"
Repatriation was always a mixed experience with many positives and negatives. Our final repatriation to Australia was particularly difficult as the whole transition took about a year before we could even start to adjust to a new life in Australia.
Toby, 30
– 15 years with a missionary organisation

> *I was overseas for the first several years of my childhood. My sister is four years older and had already had some years at school in Australia before we moved, so she had friends to return to. I had to start entirely fresh while the kids around me already had established friendships at school.*
> Rosie, 25
> – 6 years with DFAT

On the other hand, repatriation is a very different move because of all the assumptions made about living 'at home' – both by the repats themselves, and the people around them after they return. For example, 45% of our cohort who experienced repatriation as children struggled to learn Australian slang, and 75% didn't understand pop culture references.

> *Being outside Australia meant I didn't learn about local music, TV, popular celebrities.*
> Derek, 45
> – 10 years with a missionary organisation

> *I was born and raised overseas – I spent none of my childhood living in Australia and I found it very challenging to adjust. I looked Australian and I had the passport, but none of the cultural references, friends, memories, etc. That was a tough transition.*
> Tamar, 50
> – 18 years in the business sector

> *Repatriation was awful. It was like being picked up out of one culture by a massive crane and just dropped into another. But everything was different: both from the country I left and within Australia during my absence.*
> Fayette, 61
> – 1 year in the education sector

During hundreds of research interviews for my (Tanya's) book *Misunderstood*, almost all Adult TCKs expressed that repatriation was the most painful experience of their international upbringing, regardless of demographics. For this reason it is important that those who have not yet repatriated prepare for this experience, and for those who have already repatriated to read accounts of others' experiences. Whatever repatriation is/was for you, you are not alone.

> **"**
> *My repatriation as a child was an experience I wouldn't wish on anybody. I wish I'd had more support. I didn't realise for years that there were other people who also went through this.*
> Zara, 19
> – 5 years with a missionary organisation

> **"**
> *I struggled with repatriation. It took me a few years to settle, and even now eight years later I still feel the effects.*
> Dayong, 29
> – 7 years with a missionary organisation

> **"**
> *I repatriated twice as a child. I was evacuated in early primary school due to the Gulf War. This repatriation was easier because my peers and I didn't really understand cultural identity, and there wasn't any bullying. But the second time I repatriated was absolutely awful. I was bullied relentlessly, and everyone was cognizant of my cultural and accent difference.*
> Darren, 38
> – 17 years in the education sector

> **"**
> *I returned to Australia in high school and over 15 years later I'm starting to realise how the complexities of being a TCK affected my repatriation experience. It was easy to see all the negatives as being the fault of Australians because I didn't understand the culture shock of returning to a 'foreign home'. It has taken me many years to feel I belong here and to make meaningful friendships.*
> Kaylee, 39
> – 6 years with a missionary organisation

"

Our family's repatriation was completely unsupported. My brother and I both took many years to process the negative aspects of our experiences and integrate our 'otherness' into our lives.
Jane, 48
– 5 years in aid and development

"

I came to Australia at 17 in order to finish high school. I struggled deeply with the transition to life here and ultimately decided to return to Hong Kong. I didn't return to Australia again until I was 23.
Tamar, 50
– 18 years in the business sector

"I Still Call Australia Home"

The song "I Still Call Australia Home" has been used in advertisements by multinational corporations for years, often featuring Australian celebrities who have long lived in other countries. Calling Australia home and feeling at home in Australia are two very different things.

"

As an adult who has lived in Sydney for over 10 years, I think I now call Australia home rather than any other place, much more so than when I was young. But I think if I moved overseas, I would be happy easily claiming a new home as well!
Toby, 30
– 15 years with a missionary organisation

"

I call Australia home because that is legally where I'm from and where I live now. I don't necessarily 'feel' Australian, but then I don't necessarily feel happy to call anywhere home.
Kaylee, 39
– 6 years with a missionary organisation

The biggest difficulty for repatriating Australians is the assumption that Australia is home. This may be somewhat true for adults who have strong ties established in Australia to which they can return. The longer a person is away from Australia, however, and the larger the percentage of their life those years represent, the less likely Australia is to feel like their home. They may know to call it their home country, but it is unlikely that strong emotional ties are in place.

If a family lives away from Australia for three years, for example, those three years form 8% of a 36-year-old parent's life. Those same three years form one-third of a nine-year-old child's life, and half their living memory. They form half of a six-year-old child's life and their entire living memory, and the whole of a three-year-old child's life.

"
I was devastated to leave the country I grew up in and cried myself to sleep every night when I moved to Australia. My sisters' situations were different, so they didn't understand. I was alone.
Annabelle, 46
– 11 years with a missionary organisation

Here is another illustration: a 28-year-old returning to Australia after seven years abroad has spent one-quarter of their life outside Australia, including almost all of their adulthood.

Keeping this in mind is important for repats of all ages and life stages. Our sense of home is all about our experiential connections and emotional ties. When we are not physically there, these connections are not being made in a consistent way.

"
Repatriation as a child was a horrible experience. Kids are cruel if you speak differently, which I did, let alone the different school systems. I was mocked every day for years. The adult experience of repatriation was 'that's nice, let's change subjects within 10 seconds and never speak of your time overseas again'. That was easier but the lack of recognition was still invalidating and damaging.
Hurley, 64
– 3 years with the ADF

A lack of these ties can also be part of a lack of identity. Repatriation can be particularly stressful for TCKs who do not identify with their passport country. Not all Australians overseas *feel* they are Australian, or identify with being Australian. TCKs who were immersed in a different culture with which they *did* feel identity and belonging will likely feel deep grief over losing this place when they repatriate.

> **"**
> *I loved my time in Papua New Guinea. It was all I knew for the first eight years of my life. PNG was full of familiar sounds and smells; it was much quieter and slower. I loved the tropical rain, the green, the food. Australia seemed bland, dead, and weird when I arrived. People did the strangest things, wore the strangest things, listened to the strangest things. I was in complete culture shock. Everyone appeared to be white. Everything seemed really loud. I missed the missionary community. I missed the Tok Pisin language. Looking at the dry land would make me angry. I would scream or cry sometimes because I was so distressed by the lack of water and green.*
> Etta, 42
> – 8 years with a missionary organisation

One key way this is expressed is in the phrases "welcome back" and "welcome home". Friends and family excited to have you home may utter these words from hearts full of love and acceptance and welcome. Many TCKs, however, find them hollow and off-putting. Being welcomed 'back' to a country you have not lived in (or do not remember living in), or welcomed 'home' while you are grieving the home you left behind, is confusing at best and painful at worst. Some TCKs use these phrases as markers of people they believe will not, or cannot, understand them – a red flag marking those who are unsafe to share their hearts with.

> **"**
> *Everyone expected me to be excited about 'coming home' to Australia, but in reality it was just another transitory stay with uncertainty, no friends, and culture shock no one understands.*
> Mei Mei, 22
> – 10 years with a missionary organisation

Rather than fitting in immediately as Australians at home, repats in general and especially repatriating TCKs are more like 'hidden immigrants' (a term coined by Pollock and Van Reken). While they possess Australian passports and may look and sound like Australians – unlike new migrants – beneath the surface they share a lot in common with non-citizen arrivals. Aspects of Australian dialect, Australian customs, social etiquette, fashion sense, road rules, and even Australian food may feel odd or perhaps uncomfortable. These things are not automatically conferred through citizenship or heritage but are learned in a community. Repatriating TCKs may need some time to adjust and learn the 'rules' of life in Australia.

Jane Barron explains it this way: "Returning 'home' after living abroad is regarded as the hardest of all international moves. Sometimes referred to as 'hidden immigrants', they suddenly find themselves wrestling with their own personal and cultural identity, usually far from family and all that is familiar. Their passport says they are Australian but alongside their domestic Australian peers they may realise they are unfamiliar with Australia and the culture. It can lead to feelings of isolation and confusion. Questions such as 'Who am I? Where do I belong? Where is home?' emerge."

"

It was an absolute culture shock coming back and going into high school. I didn't know how to talk to kids my age. I completely missed those two years of socialisation around 12–13 years of age. It took me about four years before I really formed close friendships after that. I had missed all pop culture references; I didn't know what everyone else liked. Re-entry was definitely the biggest challenge that I faced.
Nathan, 28
– 5 years with a missionary organisation

"

There were several cultural dynamics at work during repatriation. Particularly for me, I was trying to understand the Australian culture but also, as a missionary kid, I had to try and understand a secular culture. On top of that, learning how to go from being homeschooled to a large public school system.
Kimberley, 35
– 7 years with a missionary organisation

Arguments for repatriation

Repatriation is hard for most TCKs – but that doesn't mean it's not worth doing. There are benefits to repatriation as well! 85% of our childhood repatriation cohort identified positives about their repatriation, including 64% who were grateful to see extended family more often. 40% enjoyed the environment in Australia, 36% enjoyed food options, and 25% even said their overseas experiences helped them make friends!

> **"**
> *It's never easy but I found that approaching repatriation with a positive attitude, even when it's usually not your choice, makes all the difference in how much you enjoy being back in your home country.*
> Jake, 19
> – 5 years with a missionary organisation

> **"**
> *I've built a career here now, made friends who are now across a few states, married and got dogs. I love the country, the bush* here in Australia. I've travelled away and then come back from overseas thinking how grateful I am to be Australian.*
> Anna, 29
> – 16 years with a missionary organisation

> **"**
> *It was my decision to come back to Australia as an adult, but not without a lot of grief and shattered dreams. It has been for good – though I didn't know that at the time.*
> Shellie, 54
> – 1 year with the ADF

There are lots of logistical benefits to living in Australia as an Australian citizen, many of which we will discuss in *Section 3* of this book. More than that, learning to live comfortably in your passport country provides you with a security net. You can then go out into the world for as long as you like, knowing that no matter what happens, you can always come back to Australia. If you lose a job – and your work visa and residency with it – Australia will always be open to you. If another global pandemic happens and borders are closing – Australia will always be an option for you. Creating roots in Australia is a beneficial thing to do for yourself and your future, no matter where you expect life to take you.

The Four Stages of Starting Again

In *Misunderstood*, I (Tanya) outlined four stages most TCKs go through when adjusting to a big change – especially repatriation. Here, we are going to adapt those four stages with reference to the Australian context specifically.

Isolation

Repatriation is an arrival – and arrival is the second half of departure. We arrive in Australia having left somewhere else, which means experiencing loss and grief. Routines and relationships have been left and lost. So have places, communities, activities, sights, sounds, smells, tastes, and comforts. It can be jarring to lose so much at once, even if you have the knowledge to understand what you are going through as well as the time and space to process it. This means the first type of isolation that is often experienced during repatriation is self-isolation – choosing not to engage, not to make connections, not to make an effort.

> **66**
> *When I moved back to Australia, I was in a small country town. I love the town and I did already have friends and family there, but it was easy to avoid meeting people my age or really people I had anything in common with. And I wanted to avoid connections. I had said goodbye to so many people every year for my whole life, and then I said goodbye to everyone all at once when I finished high school and moved to Australia. It was too much, and I didn't want to say more goodbyes. The only way to avoid that is to avoid building deep, important relationships. So I avoided making friends; this lasted 18 months.*
> Katie, 24
> – 14 years with a missionary organisation

Isolation can also feel imposed from the outside. When first arriving in Australia, it is common to feel misunderstood and overlooked by Australian peers. People around you may not know much about where you previously lived – the city, country, or entire region! You may deal with negative stereotypes about a place that is important to you – the reverse of dealing with Australian stereotypes while living abroad. Often, these stereotypes cut deeper, as they come at the time you are dealing with the grief of leaving that place and losing those people.

> **"**
> *I didn't realise that there was little public interest or recognition of what happens overseas (or as much as I was used to, while living overseas). That was difficult to cope with!*
> Andrew, 34
> – 8 years for family reasons, 9 years in the education/business sectors

> **"**
> *There is certainly a lingering idea of exoticism that is pinned on a person during repatriation. If you've lived abroad for a time, you attract curiosity but struggle to connect deeply unless they have also had cross-cultural exposure.*
> Kimberley, 35
> – 7 years with a missionary organisation

> **"**
> *I lived in a profoundly different culture outside Australia. Repatriation as a child was isolating. I didn't fit in and had difficulty making friends. I also had difficulty maintaining friendships overseas, which caused profound distress when I was unable to make friends in Australia. This was isolating and created depression, anxiety, and loneliness.*
> Jesse, 38
> – 3 years with a missionary organisation

It is also common to find that people do not want to hear your stories, which is another kind of pain. Sometimes this happens because they cannot relate to your stories. Another particularly Australian reason for this is tall poppy syndrome*: the need Australians have to tear down those perceived to be overly prideful. If your new peers have never left the country, they may feel your stories of life overseas are a form of boasting, and tease you for them. Whether this is deliberately mean or gentle teasing intended to be affectionate, it can be devastating for repatriating TCKs. Two-thirds of our childhood repatriation cohort felt they couldn't share an important part of their life with others, and one-third said they were perceived as 'arrogant' when they tried. (We'll talk more about Australian arrogance in *Chapter 7*.)

A common temptation is to lean into the sense of isolation: to want nothing to do with these rude people and isolate yourself further. While tempting, this stalls the process of adapting and starting again.

> **"**
> *Losing time, place, culture, and friends while a teenager at the same time as tackling senior high school and career prospects was very hard, and without close, understanding, supportive circles of people and individuals, I am pretty sure I would have entered depression.*
> Anna, 29
> – 16 years with a missionary organisation

Investment

The second stage of starting again is investment. This is all about getting involved: joining groups and clubs and teams, spending time with people through activities, and just hanging out. It doesn't sound hard, at least on the surface, but 60% of our cohort struggled with the difference in how friendships were made and maintained.

> **"**
> *I had great difficulty making friends as a young teen when I came back because I did not fit in and I had virtually no shared interests or experiences with my peers. It took about three years for me to make close friendships with the other kids in school, just in time for us all to graduate.*
> Nathan, 28
> – 5 years with a missionary organisation

The first thing to keep in mind is that in most Australian communities, a lot of extracurricular activities are linked to community organisations rather than to schools. That is, students who are really into sport are likely to play for a local community 'club' rather than for their school (with the exception of some private schools). The same goes for music, art, and other pursuits. This means that these activities are not always 'built in' to the school community, and finding the best place to join in may take a little more searching. This can often be difficult for families leaving international communities where most of their social and extracurricular needs were met within the school community. The good thing about this is it gives you an additional pool of people to get involved with – more places where you can potentially find friends.

> **"**
> *It was really hard coming back to Australia! But I think getting involved with the school really helped. The biggest thing would have to be the sport and music groups I was a part of.*
> Milly, 21
> – 10 years for family reasons

The goal of investment is to put your time in, trusting that it will pay dividends later. Try lots of things, meet lots of people, sign up for every activity, and hopefully you'll find some that suit you!

Tips for getting involved

1. **Find contacts in your local area before you move**
   Look into options to connect online – find out what exists and get some options on your calendar. Most local clubs have Facebook groups, which can be a good place to start.

2. **Join a community group**
   You can also get involved by joining a religious community, a volunteer organisation, a community choir or orchestra, a book club, a knitting group, a board game event – anything you like doing, you can probably find other people doing together.

   > **"**
   > *Getting involved with the Christian group at uni was a big part of making it easier and where I made most of my close friendships here. My biggest fear was that I'd never have good friends that really understood me like I did at school in India. But it turned out not to be true. I do have friends that know and understand me.*
   > Tara, 37
   > – 18 years with a missionary organisation

3. Sport is huge
Sport is one of the fastest ways to connect in Australia – there are lots of options! (We talk more about sport in *Chapter 7*.)

4. Try something new
The most common pastimes in Australia may be very different to what was common where you lived previously. Even within Australia there can be big differences from place to place when it comes to common sports to play/watch and other extracurricular activities. 46% of our childhood repatriation cohort struggled with the difference in sports and other activities. Getting involved may mean giving new activities a chance.

5. Advertise your interests
Another way to connect is to let people find you: advertise your interests with stickers or clothing logos that will be meaningful to people who share the same interest.

"

Getting involved in Australian life was very hard. I had lived my most formative years (age 10–17) overseas. I left behind my friends, including my boyfriend. I initially referred to Australians as 'them' and 'they', not including myself as an Australian. I had not wanted to return to Australia at the time. It helped if I did not refer to having lived overseas. Once I had had holidays in Australia that I could talk about, people seemed happy to listen to me if I spoke to them about Australian experiences. I seemed to get on better with overseas students or people from regional areas.
Sally, 52
– 7 years with a missionary organisation

Getting involved doesn't mean you will like everything you try or everyone you meet. It's just about getting out there! If you don't try things, you have no chance to meet new people and gain new interests. Sometimes the activities you try may not seem terribly interesting in themselves but will be a good way to meet people. Sometimes you'll find an activity you really enjoy! Either way, it's an investment success.

66
Something I share with teens in the early stages of repatriation is that 'There are really good things about Australia. There are things you'll learn here, even though you're grieving the place you've left.' I wish I could tell them, 'This way that you look at other cultures – where you're really open and keen to learn – maybe you should bring that point of view towards Australia and your Australian friends and Australian practices. Instead of passing judgement and being critical, maybe you can bring that kind of openness and willingness to learn our own passport culture.'
Lucy, 38
– 9 years with a missionary organisation

Enjoyment

For Investment to progress to Enjoyment, the effort you put into meeting people and making connections must become a two-way street. That is, there must be people reaching out to you and taking an interest in you. Enjoyment happens when we truly engage – when we have shared our true selves with others, have been known and accepted by them, and truly enjoy these connections.

Some TCKs have trouble believing they will get to this point in Australia with people who have not shared their childhood experiences. It does often take a few years. This is particularly hard if you have always had short-term friendships before, whether because you moved frequently, or others moved away from you. The idea that it takes a few years to develop a friendship in Australia, when a few years was the total length of a friendship in your international life, can be very daunting!

66
I had to adjust to long-term relationships after short-term relationships, but I've never seen anyone talk about this.
Amy, 23
– 12 years with a missionary organisation

One of the best reasons to get involved in lots of activities when you first arrive in Australia is that it means as you find the activities that do not suit you, and the people who show no interest in getting to know you further, you can drop out of those activities while still having others you can continue to pursue.

> **"**
> *Attending church youth group and social hangouts with youth group members and leaders helped me make friends and feel a part of the community. It took a year and a half to feel like I had close friends. Lots of camping for fun, general shenanigans, and spontaneous adventures with friends (and my parents allowing me to partake in those) helped to form good memories and build relationships.*
> Anna, 29
> – 16 years with a missionary organisation

One of the most common ways Australian adults will begin the process of getting to know each other better is by inviting you out for a drink, often after the conclusion of an activity. Going for drinks at the pub* after a game (whether you are watching or playing) is a very common Australian social activity. It can also be confronting for TCKs who did not grow up in drinking cultures. We'll talk more about Australia's drinking culture in *Chapter 6*, but for now what matters is that 'going to the pub*' does not mean you have to drink alcohol; nor does it mean people intend to get drunk. Often each person will have one or two drinks while chatting amiably, then go home. Skipping these invitations often means missing the opportunity to develop real friendships alongside an activity.

Tips for engaging well

1. **Two-way street**
    Focus on connections that provide a 'two-way street' – where the other person shares some of their story, and also leaves space for you to share some of your story. Get there by sharing small pieces of your story, and asking questions about theirs. Start with smaller and more 'surface' aspects of life (see the 'Small Talk' section in *Chapter 7* for ideas) before getting into more meaningful topics.

2. **Share your true self**
    To engage well, you need to share your true self – not create

a persona that fits in with what you think is expected. This can be a little scary if 'fitting in' has been your comfort zone in the past, but rather than changing yourself to fit in with 20 people, find the 3 people you can be real with.

3. **Make memories**

    A great way to bond with people is to make memories together. Whether you do something fun, bougie, scary, adventurous, or plain dumb, do things together that will become stories you tell for years to come!

Even when engagement goes perfectly, there is no guarantee you'll get to 'keep' these new Australian friends, either. But engaging to the point of enjoyment means you have witnesses to this season of your life – you are not alone, and you will have people to remember this time with in the future.

> **"**
> *Despite my efforts to keep these people at arm's length, they worked their way closer and closer and became good friends. For the first year I was still a bit guarded and didn't let anyone get really close. But then an acquaintance became a housemate, who became a truly close friend, and I let myself open my heart to her in a way I had so wanted to avoid because of how much goodbye would hurt. Then she dragged more friends into our little group, wonderful girls who are very dear friends now as well. It took me about three years in Australia to get to that point. It was worth it. I wouldn't trade my new friends for anything. But I was right that saying goodbye to them would hurt.*
> Katie, 24
> – 14 years with a missionary organisation

Settling

Settling is the final stage of starting again. This is when you are comfortable saying 'I live here' without needing to qualify that. Settling does *not* mean you must feel entirely at home, that it is your only home, that you must not love anywhere else, or that you will never want to live anywhere else. But it means you have found a way to be comfortable where you are, and to be *present*. To live where you are.

> **"**
> *My first home will always be Papua New Guinea, and the identity from that runs deep and will never be lost. I knew I was meant to build foundations here in Australia for now, so that's what I've done. I'd love to live overseas again, but I've put down some good roots here and uprooting from relationships would be hard; it always is.*
> Anna, 29
> – 16 years with a missionary organisation

> **"**
> *Australia started to feel like home when I bought my house. Well, maybe after the second year. I think it always takes two years for me to feel comfortable in a place.*
> Siew Ling, 38
> – 16 years for family reasons

The word 'settling' can be scary to some TCKs. The idea of settling in Australia can be particularly scary to many Australian TCKs. But settling does not have to be permanent. It is a state of mind that says you are open to staying. Most importantly, living settled in a place means you make it your home as long as you are there. When you have an opportunity to live in Australia, make the most of it. Enjoy the work you have, the relationships in your life, and anything else that marks your life here.

> **"**
> *I feel settled in Australia, to some extent. There is definitely still 'the bug' to move and travel and live overseas. I have been back several years now, longer than our last stint overseas. I've just started working full-time and that seems to tie me here more than I had thought.*
> Claire, 27
> – 9 years with a missionary organisation

"
I think raising children in Australia has played a big part in my ability to feel settled here. I have good friends and have been able to establish a business here, so I definitely feel like I have planted roots here finally.
Tamar, 50
– 18 years in the business sector

"
I have settled. I made the mental decision that my home was where I hung my hat up. I sought to not move for the past 19 years – after more than 20 moves in the previous 30 years! It is still interesting how I feel really happy amongst Spanish-speakers. I am part of a group that meets each month to speak in Spanish and I make the most of every opportunity to speak it when I can.
Sally, 52
– 7 years with a missionary organisation

Chapter 6:

Australian Culture

In this section we will go over a lot of things that might seem small and unimportant but which, when added up, make mainstream Australian culture what it is. Some might feel so natural and normal you wonder why they're here. Others might feel completely weird and unnatural. Hopefully you will learn a bit about what Australians think is 'normal' and the 'why' behind this. We quote several times from the SBS* Cultural Atlas of Australian Culture, which is a great resource for learning more about mainstream Australian culture, as well as norms for Indigenous Australian cultures. Learn more at culturalatlas.sbs.com.au/australian-culture

Multiculturalism

Most of Australia prides itself on being a multicultural country. As of March 2023, the Australian population stands at 26.4 million people. Nearly 30% of Australians were born overseas. The top 10 countries where overseas-born Australians are most likely to originate from are England, India, China, New Zealand, the Philippines, Vietnam, South Africa, Italy, Malaysia, and Sri Lanka. In the 15 years prior to the COVID-19 pandemic, there was an average net gain of about two hundred thousand new migrants to Australia per year. (More information about Australia can be learned at the Australian Bureau of Statistics (ABS) website: abs.gov.au)

In addition, as Professor Greg Noble from the Institute for Culture and Society at Western Sydney University says, "Federal and state governments spend hundreds of millions of dollars each year on substantial programs – on learning English as a further language, community language programs, interpreting and translation services, community organisation support, funding for community arts, and so on."

"
We are a genuinely multicultural country – one of the most multicultural in the world. This has been an explicit government policy for decades. I think it's made us a much more culturally rich country but it is not without problems.
Shellie, 54
– 1 year with the ADF

Unfortunately, Australia's brand of multiculturalism often seems skin-deep. Anglo-Australian culture embraces different cuisines, different skin tones, and perhaps different clothing and languages – but not necessarily different worldviews. As Monica Deng – Adult TCK, immigrant to Australia, and president of South Sudanese Australian Youth United (SSAYU) – says, "Harmonious coexistence, where diversity is ingrained in the very fabric of Australian society, remains an aspiration that awaits fulfilment."

This can be disheartening for TCKs in particular, but it is not the whole story. Greg Noble also says, "Australian multiculturalism is often superficial, focusing on the trivial and banal aspects of ethnic difference that can, for example, easily be celebrated or consumed. In schools we tend to opt for the multicultural day rather than deep and sustained programs of engaging with difference. But we shouldn't simply dismiss all multicultural programs as a result."

"
To be honest, if a white person tells you that Australia is a multicultural society, they're probably just talking about the food options!
Cardamon, 23
– 11 years in aid and development

"
It took me a long time to figure out what disappointed me so much about multiculturalism in Australia. I imagined something like my international school: people from dozens of different cultures who worked together to figure out our own cultural paradigm (part of the Third Culture). Some cultures had more influence than others, but there were real meaningful interactions between cultures and no one could just assume that their own

cultural norms applied. It doesn't work like that in Australia. Most white Australians think multiculturalism is achieved when there are people around with lots of different skin colours and maybe some food or music or dances from different countries. They have no concept of culture extending to how people think and communicate and fundamentally see the world. White Australian culture is the dominant culture and the cultural paradigm the country operates in, and I don't think most white Australians are even aware of that.
Katie, 24
– 14 years with a missionary organisation

"It took me ten years to understand that Australia is not Canada and Perth is not Toronto," says Dr Danau Tanu, anthropologist and author of *Growing Up in Transit.* "The common language can be deceiving. I expected the same level of multiculturalism I had found in Canada, and was disappointed. When I recalibrated my expectations it was easier."

This can also cause a lot of stress for Australians who have cultural heritage from other parts of the world, and feel pressure to perform to different cultural expectations at home and in 'Australian' public (such as at school/work). Australian TCKs may also feel pressure to create an 'Aussie' persona that is far from their true self – perhaps including an 'Aussie' name. Those choosing to live as their integrated selves may be hurt when they are misunderstood or made fun of, but performing for mainstream Anglo-Australian culture also takes a toll.

As Dr Danau Tanu explains, "Anglo people like to say 'I don't see colour' because they think racism is using the 'n word' when you see a black person, but in Australia we accept people looking different – as long as they all think the same. When we perform Anglo culture, we enable these people to say 'I don't see colour' because isn't it nice that all these people look different and get along. The problem is when the Anglo person doesn't recognise that the people of colour are doing all the work of cultural adjustment."

There has been progress over time. As Monica Deng says, "I cannot deny the progress we have made in embracing multiculturalism. The once-distant dream of fostering an inclusive Australia has gradually become a tangible reality. We are a nation constantly evolving, continually learning from our past and striving towards a future where diversity is not just tolerated but cherished. Yes, we have come a long way, but the journey towards embracing multiculturalism in Australia is far from over."

Greg Noble adds, "There are many migrants who have quite a deep and passionate commitment to multiculturalism because, rightly or wrongly, they see it as recognising them. So they invest a lot of time and effort in it. But this doesn't deny the fact that much of what is done in the name of multiculturalism is trivial."

We make meaning through our actions. Growing numbers of Australians value true cultural exchange – want to learn, and are willing to change. But there are still those who are not interested in understanding the cultural complexities of lives lived between nations.

> **"**
> *I am Australian, but I wish Australia would accept me as an Australian. Ironically, Australia bills itself as 'multicultural', a nation of immigrants and welcoming of new immigrants. But my ancestors are Australian. I have made a pilgrimage to Gallipoli. But none of this means anything as I am still the 'bloody* Yank*' to other Australians.*
> Darren, 38
> – 17 years in the education sector

So what is an Australian TCK to do? There is no magic solution, but there are some things that help. The first is acknowledging that Australians are a mixed bunch. Some Australians who pride themselves on the country's 'multiculturalism' aren't overly interested in understanding different cultural worldviews. Some Australians think they live in a multicultural society, but don't realise those other cultural worldviews exist. Some Australians, however, are very interested in learning from others – and are willing to be quiet long enough to listen. Each group requires a different approach.

Connecting with different types of Australians

1. **Interested**
   With new Australian acquaintances who are interested in your international experiences, it's fairly easy to connect! As long as there's mutual give-and-take in the friendship, you'll have a chance to share your point of view, including cultural nuances from your experiences.

2. **Willing to learn**
   With Australians who appreciate multiculturalism while remaining ignorant of the vast differences in cultural worldviews, there are ways to introduce them gradually. My (Tanya's) favourite approach is what I call 'giving a taste' – both literally and figuratively. Literally, I make food from a place, and use it as a stepping stone to discuss aspects of culture, in small doses. People like to eat, and food becomes a vehicle for sharing stories and cultural insights. Figuratively, I try not to overwhelm people. If they only have a cup-full of curiosity, throwing a big bucket of information at them is overwhelming, and may stop them engaging again in the future.

3. **Uninterested**
   For those who aren't interested at all, the simplest strategy for moving a step closer is reciprocating understanding. This is where you invest time in understanding their worldview and perspective. What was it like for them, growing up how they did, where they did? Often, investing time in listening to these stories with genuine interest creates opportunities for you to share pieces of your own stories as well. That said, you are never obligated to invest in a relationship with anyone who dismisses your experiences and the things that matter to you.

66

My father is Indian, my mother is Dutch-Australian, I was born in Brazil, and my family settled in Australia. Over time while travelling I realised that Australia is home because it is the one place that truly accepts me for who I am.

> *Overseas, everyone would say, 'Where are you actually from?' because no Australians are brown as far as they're concerned. In Australia I still get the 'go back to where you came from' nonsense, but Australia is the only place in the world where I truly feel like I belong. It's not that people with my sort of story and background are 'normal', but it's accepted.*
> Nathan, 28
> – 5 years with a missionary organisation

Racism

Racism against BIPOC (Black, Indigenous, and people of colour) also exists in Australia, both in microaggressions and in outright aggression. This is an ongoing issue that needs to be dealt with in Australian society. Racism and racist microaggressions are more prevalent among white Australians who did not grow up in diverse communities.

Dr Danau Tanu explains the difference between 'overt' and 'covert' racism this way: "What I struggle with the most as a 'model minority' Asian is I don't receive overt racism. Instead it is covert – microaggressions. When racism is covert, I second-guess myself, wondering if it was really racism. Would my Anglo-Australian friends be treated the same way?"

"

> *I experienced quite a bit of racial bullying in my Australian primary school, so that probably contributed to my feeling disconnected from Australia. After being away for two years, things changed. There were more non-white people – we weren't the only ones whenever we went out. I never experienced direct racism in my Australian high school. But it was still definitely something – grappling with what my identity was, being a brown guy in a white culture. Being told to 'go back to where I came from' because I was not white was a barrier to reintegrating into society here. The ongoing racism and public discourse about immigrants in Australia impacted my Australian identity.*
> Nathan, 28
> – 5 years with a missionary organisation

Monica Deng shares the impact of her experiences of racism while attending school in Australia: "Growing up, I stood head and shoulders above my classmates, not only in physical stature but also in the richness of my dark complexion. In a sea of faces that differed from mine, I felt an acute sense of insecurity, a constant reminder that I was different. Racism slithered its way into the hallways of my schools and lurked within the public spaces I frequented. It whispered venomous words, subtly corroding my self-worth and casting shadows upon my capabilities. I was perpetually reminded of my 'luck' to be here, as if my presence itself was an act of charity."

66
There's plenty of overt racism – people saying bigoted things to or about other ethnic groups. There are also racist policies dressed up in all sorts of other language, such as the way we treat asylum seekers or fail to build systems that serve Indigenous people. I think one of the most insidious things is a bias against people who are socio-economically disadvantaged. Indigenous people and new immigrants are particularly vulnerable to the causes of socio-economic disadvantage due to systemic racism both now and historically.
Katie, 24
– 14 years with a missionary organisation

66
I routinely witness racism in my work (maternal health), and being Jewish, I am aware of rising antisemitism in this country as well. We have a BIG problem with racism in Australia, and of course, that includes our ongoing treatment of our First Nations people.
Tamar, 50
– 18 years in the business sector

Encountering racism can be stressful, especially if it happens frequently. Microaggressions can leave you questioning encounters, wondering if you would have been treated differently if you had a different skin tone or different accent. This can be particularly disheartening if you were looking forward to being 'normal' in your passport country.

> **"**
>
> *Being 'Australian' to me is steeped in racism and discrimination. I distinctly remember being told I wasn't 'Australian' if I spoke without an Australian accent.*
>
> Rosie, 25
> – 6 years with DFAT

> **"**
>
> *Growing up biracial in Malaysia we were always 'the white kids'. Coming to Australia as a 16-year-old, I thought that as 'the white kid' I was going to fit straight in. But the white kids in rural Australia saw us as foreigners.*
>
> Siew Ling, 38
> – 16 years for family reasons

"It took me ten years to operate in the Anglo-Australian cultural communication style," says Dr Danau Tanu. "I learned to ask Australians about things that interested them, and listen to their stories, and to imitate the way they interacted with each other. Before then, I had experiences of covert racism about once a week. I never knew when it would happen, so I always had to be prepared. Once I learned to talk to Anglo-Australians in a way that didn't 'trigger' them, I didn't experience covert racism so often, and I was better equipped to deal with it. Learning to apply the word 'trigger' to racist microaggressions was also really helpful for me."

Dealing with racism

A few things to keep in mind:

1. **Use discernment**
   There is a difference between innocent ignorance and malicious aggression. A person who is ignorant but open to learning may ask questions that are comfortable to answer, opening a fruitful dialogue. Dialogue is not possible with a person who has no intention to learn.

   Dr Danau Tanu explains how she deals with questions: "Australia's migration history is relatively new and there are people who don't have much experience engaging with people from different cultural backgrounds. They haven't had the opportunities and experiences that I have. They may ask ignorant questions, but they're trying to be nice and engage. There is space here for us to let go of our prejudices against them. I have more patience with people who are older, for example. Unpacking my internalised racism was also important."

2. **You can walk away**

   You are not obligated to receive racist aggression from anyone. You can walk away without explanation at any time, and you do not have to maintain contact with anyone who treats you that way. If it happens in a school/work setting, you can report the person to an authority. You also do not owe answers about your life to anyone, whether friend or stranger.

3. **You belong**

   You belong in Australia, no matter what an innocently ignorant or maliciously racist person might think – or cause you to think. One way to counter the stress of racist treatment is to enjoy everything this country has to offer you.

Dealing with racism as an Anglo-Australian

For those who have inherent privilege – especially those who are accepted as part of mainstream Anglo culture – it is important to actively speak up against racism, in both its overt and covert forms.

"
   I have seen and experienced racism on multiple occasions. Mostly just in comments or misunderstanding of someone else's culture. I think it is important that we speak out about it and continue to discuss it with our peers.
   Milly, 21
   – 10 years for family reasons

1. **Don't turn a blind eye**

   If you hear a racist comment/joke made by a friend/family member or colleague, challenge it. One of the simplest ways to do this is to calmly say: "I didn't understand that; can you explain it to me?" Ask for the comment to be repeated (say you couldn't hear), or ask what made the joke funny. Being required to explain it clearly makes most people feel uncomfortable about the casual racism they are displaying.

"
Stereotype assumptions and turning a blind eye is a common show of racism in Australia. Choose to be a steady, calm voice that makes others question their assumptions and stereotypes in conversations. Show your own compassion with simple acts of kindness, not with fanfare but unwavering in what you believe is right.
Anna, 29
– 16 years with a missionary organisation

2. Include others

A common form of 'passive' racism is not inviting certain people to events, with a baseless assumption that they won't enjoy the activity – or not noticing that they aren't included. Be deliberate in your event invites. Invite, invite, invite – make sure everyone knows they are welcome and wanted. Then look around – who is at after-work drinks, and who isn't? Who is invited to social events, and who isn't? Suggest activities everyone will enjoy – and be proactive about finding out what those activities are.

"
I've seen a lot of racism in Australia and it is embarrassing. To me the best response is to set a good example in welcoming and being friendly to people from overseas.
Marco, 64
– 11 years with a missionary organisation, 5 years with the ADF

3. Be kind

It's simple advice, but being kind to others always goes a long way. When you have inherent privilege in a society, it is even more important to make sure you notice others and show kindness.

4. **Emphasise what you have in common**
When we look at what we have in common, it brings us together. Keeping the focus on what we share with each other helps bridge gaps, engage empathy, and disempower prejudices.

66
I have definitely seen racism in Australia over the almost 50 years since I returned, in school and throughout society. The way to counter racism is to draw out the commonalities, not differences.
David, 61
– 6 years in aid and development

Respect

Every culture puts a priority on respect, but how respect is shown varies wildly from one place to another. This section shares a few tips on how respect is shown in Australian culture.

66
'Politeness and respect' in Australia are very different to what I knew as a child growing up in Hong Kong. Australians can be polite and respectful, but often I feel that it comes across as rather superficial. It's not the cultural norm as it is in many Asian cultures.
Tamar, 50
– 18 years in the business sector

66
Politeness and respect in Australia can often be indirect and invisible. Avoidance can be a feature.
David, 61
– 6 years in aid and development

Politeness is a key way to show respect in Australia. This includes using the words "please" and "thank you" liberally, even to close friends and family. Failing to say thank you is a sign of rudeness, and lack of respect. You should thank your waiter, your taxi driver, your children – anyone and everyone. Observing people around you will show you that not everyone does this, but it is extremely common – and it is a key marker of how polite (and therefore how respectful) a person is.

Australian egalitarianism

On a global scale, Australia is a highly egalitarian culture. This means that people from all walks of life are considered equal, no matter their age, gender, or profession. While there are genuine inequalities in Australian society, these are considered problems in need of solutions – the ideal is for people to be treated equally.

There *are* social classes in Australia; indeed, research by Dr Jill Sheppard and Dr Nicholas Biddle at the Australian National University demonstrated five distinct social classes within Australian society, though in a flatter social structure than is seen elsewhere in the world. As Sheppard and Biddle write: "[Australian] social classes are more inclusive than their British counterparts. There is a broader range of people, in terms of economic, social, and cultural capital in each of the Australian classes... Australian society is less hierarchical and more egalitarian than British society." (Read more in their ABC* article 'Is Australia as egalitarian as we think it is?' – see link in the *Resources* section at the back of this book.)

Greg Noble explains: "Australia sees itself as a highly egalitarian society, free of the class and other inequalities found in many parts of the world. But in fact there are enormous inequalities in wealth, access to services such as education and health, and so on. It is just that the codes of class and caste are not as entrenched or rigid as they may be in some other countries. The public ethos of equality, fairness and respect is sometimes real, and sometimes a façade."

"
Politeness and respect can be more casual in Australia than it is demonstrated in other cultures, with less ceremony. Demarcation of roles, with inherent respect, is also less defined.
Rho, 60+
– 2 years in aid and development

In Australia, respect is not granted on the basis of age, gender, or title. Respect is shown to people who are younger than you, and people you employ. Women are equal to men and should be treated as such – "capable individuals who can help themselves" (SBS Cultural Atlas).

That said, you can always help a friend out, no matter their gender – that's just being a mate!

> **"**
> *For Australians, politeness is more about attitude. It's polite to be friendly, not stand-offish, and have an attitude of being on the same level as other people. When in some cultures it might be polite to use titles, in Australian culture (particularly amongst younger people), it's almost rude to be overly formal. It doesn't convey respect so much as distance and condescension.*
> Katie, 24
> – 14 years with a missionary organisation

Another outworking of Australia's egalitarian culture is that queuing is calm and orderly. Each person is served in the order they arrived, without preference shown. Always wait your turn; do not mill around and do not cut in line ahead of someone else. If you are unsure if another person is waiting to be served, it is completely fine to ask them. If a lot of people have been milling around (such as checking out the flavours of ice cream available while waiting to be served), keep an eye on who was in front of you when you entered so you don't accidentally take their place. If a server comes to you, check that the other person has been served first.

Body etiquette

Direct eye contact is considered polite in Australia, and is often interpreted as a sign of friendliness, interest, respect, and even honesty. The SBS Cultural Atlas says this about eye contact in Australia: "Eye contact should be maintained directly as it translates sincerity, trustworthiness and approachability. However, it is important to break eye contact intermittently as holding it for prolonged periods can make Australians feel uncomfortable. When talking to a group, be sure to make equal eye contact with all people present. Conversely, Aboriginal Australians are more likely to divert their eyes during communication."

Not all Australians enjoy eye contact, but it is a mainstream norm by which people are often judged nonetheless. I (Tanya) am autistic, and I do not find eye contact comfortable. I have learned that it is a way I am judged in mainstream Australian culture, but when I am with people who know me well, I can be more relaxed.

> **"**
> *In Cambodia, making sustained eye contact, especially with someone you need to show respect to, is rude. In Australia, 'good' eye contact is polite, a sign of friendliness, openness and sincerity. This is so ingrained that it is part of mental health assessments (not that this is unreasonable, but it needs to be interpreted with caution across cultures). When I was younger, I just couldn't do eye contact the Australian way and it actually annoyed my grandfather. I now manage eye contact well enough but still need to make a conscious effort when talking to someone older than me or who outranks me at work. It feels uncomfortable to me, but I have to gauge it off how the other person seems to feel about it.*
> Katie, 24
> – 14 years with a missionary organisation

Australians tend to prefer a lot of personal space. They will stay as far from each other as possible in public spaces, such as waiting rooms and public transport. Sitting too near a stranger is considered weird, or even creepy. Even close friends often leave some space. Again, from the SBS Cultural Atlas: "Australians usually keep about an arm's length distance between one another when talking, and sometimes a little extra between men and women depending on how well they know each other."

It is unusual for platonic friends to hold hands in Australia; this is generally considered a romantic gesture. From the SBS Cultural Atlas: "People tend not to touch one another much during communication unless they are close friends. Touching someone on the shoulder or arm to emphasise a point is generally acceptable, but can otherwise be seen as a sexual advance."

Bodily functions are generally considered rude, though less so among younger generations and much less so among close friends. For this reason, it is rude to burp, fart, or spit in public. Hiccups are not rude – just annoying for the person who has them! Coughs and sneezes, while not rude in public in themselves, should always be covered by a tissue/ handkerchief or into your elbow (not your hand/s). It is also okay to blow your nose in public, as long as you use a tissue/handkerchief; it is also best to attempt to be as quiet as possible. Clean and safe public toilet blocks are provided in most public areas so that everyone has access to a private place for all kinds of bodily functions.

Outdoor life

Australia is the driest inhabited continent in the world; about 40% of Australia is covered in sand dunes. According to DCCEEW (the Department of Climate Change, Energy, the Environment and Water), 70% of Australia is classed as arid or semi-arid (receiving fewer than 350 mm of rain per year), and about 81% is classed as "rangelands" – colloquially known as the 'outback*'. On the other hand, more than 85% of Australia's population live within 50 km of the coast!

This leads to a saying in Australia: 'you are either near the water or the desert'. Perhaps you are a short drive away from the beach, or a short drive away from nature reserves in which you can go hiking. Short by Australian standards, at least!

When the weather is good, Australians love to get outside. There are lots of ways to enjoy the Australian outdoors. If you live in the tropical north (46% of Australia falls inside the tropic of Capricorn), summer might send you inside and winter is beach weather. If you live in the cooler south, winter is for rugging up* fireside and summer is for sunning yourself. Wherever you live, outdoor life is a key part of Australian culture. Learning to engage with Australia's natural environment is a great way to connect with your Australian heritage.

> **"**
> *I am not a huge lover of the great outdoors, no doubt due to the fact that I grew up in a concrete jungle. Saying that, I do appreciate how beautiful Australia is.*
> Tamar, 50
> – 18 years in the business sector

> **"**
> *Connecting with nature and natural beauty made settling easier in Australia.*
> Rho, 60+
> – 2 years in aid and development

Many of the Australian TCKs interviewed for this book talked about Australia's natural beauty being the best thing about living here. We (Kath and Tanya) both recommend trying some different ways to enjoy the Australian outdoors as part of your repatriation experience.

Ways to experience nature in Australia:

♦ Swimming in lakes, rivers, and at beaches
♦ Water sports including kayaking, fishing, surfing, boating, and many more
♦ Setting up a shade tent to spend a whole day outside, perhaps at the beach
♦ Hiking and bushwalking, often in national parks
♦ Picnics in pretty places – bring a blanket, or use free picnic tables
♦ Barbecues – in the backyard, or at many free public barbecue facilities
♦ Playing sport – or watching others play – rain or shine
♦ Camping, or visiting caravan parks; glamping is a fancier way to get outdoors!
♦ Bonfires at night in cooler places

"
I regularly do outdoor activities like bushwalking*/hikes, camping, visiting the beach, and going to dog parks.
Anna, 29
– 16 years with a missionary organisation

Sun safety

Sun safety is incredibly important in Australia as Australia has some of the highest levels of UV (ultraviolet) light in the world. Australia receives 15% more UV light during summer than Europe does. UV radiation in Australian summer is so strong that sunburn can occur in as little as 11 minutes. The Australian Bureau of Meteorology (BOM) provides a UV index to show the intensity of UV light around the country throughout the day (bom.gov.au/uv). Their forecasts include a recommendation for when sun protection is required, and the highest UV rating expected for the day.

66
I wear a hat and sunnies* if I'm in the sun, and if the sun is late morning to late afternoon I wear sunscreen.
Anna, 29
– 16 years with a missionary organisation

66
I 100% take good care of my skin here in Australia – the sun and UV rays are ferocious!
Tamar, 50
– 18 years in the business sector

Wearing (and reapplying) sunscreen is very important for avoiding sunburn, and later, skin cancers. Use SPF 30+ sunscreen and reapply every two hours. Many Australians also use rashguards* ('rashies') to cover skin during long periods in the water. These long-sleeved swimwear tops provide extra sun protection. Many are made with SPF-protective fabrics.

66
I wear sunscreen fairly often, but I also often underestimate how long I'll be in the sun and get sunburnt.
Katie, 24
– 14 years with a missionary organisation

66
I love the beach. Swimming in the ocean, walking on the sand. I am very careful about the sun. It was drilled into me to be wary of getting burnt. As a result I tend to enjoy the great outdoors early in the day and in the late afternoon.
Alice, 52
– 8 years with DFAT

A common Aussie saying taught to children is 'slip, slop, slap'; it stands for 'slip on a shirt, slop on some sunscreen, and slap on a hat'. It was a successful health campaign launched by the Australian Cancer Council in 1981 in an attempt to lower Australia's high rates of skin cancer. One version adds 'wrap' at the end, for wrapping on a pair of sunglasses, and the current version is 'slip, slop, slap, seek, slide' including seeking shade and sliding on sunglasses. There is a colourful mural of this slogan (complete with sun safety-conscious animals) on the wall next to the playground I (Tanya) take my nephews to play at.

> **"**
> *I am very sun safety conscious. Many friends have skin cancers. So yes to hat and sunscreen, long sleeves, collars, etc.*
> Hurley, 64
> – 3 years with the ADF

Punctuality

Most Australians are pretty punctual most of the time – especially in the cities. You should aim to be early for all your official appointments; sometimes being just five minutes late may mean you'll lose your spot. Often you will be expected to fill in paperwork before your appointment begins, so a good rule of thumb is to arrive 10–15 minutes before your appointment is scheduled to begin. While some offices (especially doctors and government departments) are notorious for running behind schedule, this is not always the case, and especially when attending a first appointment at a new office, it is better to be early than late.

> **"**
> *My husband and I often run late for social things. Work and more official events should be punctual.*
> Anna, 29
> – 16 years with a missionary organisation

When meeting friends

If someone says they will meet you at 8:00 pm, they will most likely be there around 8:00–8:10 pm. If you are invited to arrive between 1:00 pm and 3:00 pm for a long gathering, you should plan to arrive between 1:15 pm and 2:45 pm.

If a family or group of friends know each other well, punctuality will usually relax over time. In any other case, it is important to be timely. While some Australians aim to be 'fashionably late' to group gatherings – preferring not to be among the first to arrive at an event

– anything outside the parameters above will tend to be remarked on negatively.

66

Australians are reasonably punctual, by world standards.
Rho, 60+
– 2 years in aid and development

66

In Australia I'm usually early or on time. In the Philippines, the relationship is more important than the time, so events start half an hour to an hour later.
Opal, 28
– 15 years with a missionary organisation

Most of the time it's okay to be early to meet friends, but if you are meeting a person at their house, try not to be more than five minutes early as they may still be preparing for your arrival. It is usually okay to be 10 to 15 minutes late to a small gathering of people. If you are meeting at a restaurant, it is important to be on time as people will wait for you to arrive before ordering their food.

If you are running late (even by 10 minutes), it is polite to call or text as soon as you realise you will not arrive at the agreed-upon time, giving an estimate of what time you will arrive. If people are meeting for a meal and you will be more than 15 minutes late, you might suggest they go ahead and order without you.

66

Australians are very punctual. Having spent a chunk of my growing up time in a 'rubber time' culture this is something I still struggle with now. I'm always late because I prioritise the people I'm with over the next place I'm going. But often Australians will be unhappy if you are more than five minutes late because here that sends the message that you are not prioritising them. That's been a lesson I've had to learn, and a balance I've had to find. I still naturally prioritise the place I'm at and often run late, but I strive not to be more than 5 to 10 minutes late if I do run late.
Kelly, 37
– 2 years with a missionary organisation

The exception to this 'rule' is big social gatherings or parties, when there are a lot of people attending. It can be acceptable to be late to these events if you know many others have arrived on time, and your host is busy with them – and therefore less likely to be waiting for you. The party will go on whether you're there on time or not! If you are coming from a culture where arriving an hour or two after a suggested time is normal, you may find yourself missing entire events, offending people, and missing out on future invitations.

> **"**
> *I'd say Australians are very punctual. Those who are not are usually from other cultures. People do get quite angry when people are not on time. I always like to run on time because it is polite.*
> Milly, 21
> – 10 years for family reasons

> **"**
> *Australians generally are punctual! I found this really hard after I returned from overseas as in South America you never arrived on time. I soon learned that people here do not wait around for 30 minutes for you to arrive!*
> Sally, 52
> – 7 years with a missionary organisation

Eating out

What to wear

Australians tend to prefer dressing down – choosing more casual clothing options when going out. In fact, as the SBS Cultural Atlas says, "Being overdressed for a gathering is sometimes considered more embarrassing than being underdressed." Even shorts and thongs* will be fine at a casual eatery. A neat pair of jeans and a nice top/shirt paired with clean shoes will be accepted at all but formal gatherings. That said, many Australians appreciate individual style. Take the time to develop a style that makes you feel comfortable as yourself.

Paying

It is normal for friends eating together to split the cost of the meal in a way that ensures each individual only pays for what they ordered. Inviting someone out to eat does not mean offering to pay for them; if you are invited out to eat, you will be expected to pay for your meal, unless they say otherwise. Australians most commonly split bills, usually sending each other money with online banking apps; third-party apps (like Venmo, WeChat, or Ko-fi) are rarely used.

> **"**
> *I don't eat out often. When I do, it's usually informal. I don't usually dress up. Australians are less likely to share multiple dishes in the middle of the table than in the country where I grew up. We usually either split payment, or if it's someone I see often, sometimes we take turns paying. When asked if we want to split the bill, there's usually a moment where we look at each other. Either someone volunteers to pay the whole bill, or the default option is to split it.*
> Katie, 24
> – 14 years with a missionary organisation

Offering to pay for the whole group at a meal is unusual and may make others uncomfortable. Each person pays for their own meal. On the other hand, groups who drink together will often take turns buying a 'round' of drinks – buying each person in the group a drink, with the understanding that others will do the same in turn. It is normal for members of a group to take turns buying 'rounds' for the group, which may occur on the same night or over several meetings. To accept free drinks in this manner while not taking a turn paying for the group is generally considered rude. When you want to take a turn buying a round, you can say "my shout" or "this round is on me."

The phrase "my shout" or "my treat" can also be used if you want to pay for a friend's meal. Another common one is "it's on me". Sometimes this will be said at the conclusion of a meal when it is time to pay. At other times, one person may choose to offer to treat the other at the beginning of the meal, when sitting down or looking at the menu.

Generosity is an important value for many Australians. To be seen as 'stingy' (someone who does not share what they have) or a 'scab' (someone who regularly gets free things from others without reciprocating) is socially unacceptable. If you spend a lot of time with a group of friends who have higher incomes than you (and who therefore want to eat out at more expensive places), it is appropriate to have a quiet one-on-one conversation with a person in the group with whom you are close, to let them know that you cannot keep up financially. If you have good friends, this will be seen as an opportunity for them to practise generosity, and not a situation where you are being 'stingy' or a 'scab' when you cannot pay as much as they can. Most good friends would rather chip in to help pay for your drinks/meal so that you can join them at the places they enjoy.

If the person with extra income is the odd one out in a group, they will chip in while being careful not to splash their cash around due to the Australian value of humility.

> **"**
> *With friends, generally you buy your own drinks and split the meal bill, commonly by one person paying on card and the rest contributing cash, but increasingly people pay electronically. If you earn more, you might be expected to pick up small tabs occasionally. I've seen someone do it as standard practice, but he was immensely tactful about it so it didn't look like he was telling everyone else he was richer than them.*
> Chris, 58
> – 1 year in the business sector

Tipping

To call over a waiter/waitress, do not wave or yell. Instead, keep an eye out for them until they make eye contact, and then nod or raise your hand. You can also gently say "excuse me" as they pass by.

Wait staff in Australia tend to be more subtle and stay out of the diners' way as much as possible. This may seem like 'bad' service if you are accustomed to very solicitous servers found in other countries (especially the USA), but Australian diners generally prefer not to be disturbed during their meal. If you need something, make eye contact and then smile, nod, or raise a hand. They will usually smile, nod, or raise a hand in response and come over to you as soon as they have a free moment. Waving or calling out in a loud/direct manner is considered rude.

Tipping is not necessary in restaurants or places of service in Australia. You never need to add an additional fee on top of a service performed for you – everything is built in. Where a service fee/gratuity is expected (usually only at high-end hotels and restaurants), this will be automatically added to the bill. Many small restaurants and cafes have tip jars on the counter; while tips are appreciated, especially if you receive a special service or it is a place you enjoy or frequent regularly, this is entirely optional and never expected.

66
I rarely tip in Australia. Only for exceptional service."
Marco, 64
– 11 years with a missionary organisation, 5 years with the ADF

Alcohol

Australia is well known for its casual drinking culture. What we mean by 'casual drinking culture' is that drinking alcohol is seen as a normal part of life that most adults take part in regularly, especially connected to social situations. Meeting friends or co-workers for drinks after work, sport, or other activities is extremely common. It is a common way to unwind after a day of work, before going home (or out) for dinner. It is rare for a party or large social gathering, including work parties, to *not* include alcoholic drinks. This is a comfortable thing for most Australians. There is also a culture of heavy drinking in some sections of Australian society, although this has diminished somewhat over time.

66
Many Australians think you can't have a good time without alcohol so it is very integrated into the culture, even for work parties. It is quite different to the country I grew up in, where alcohol is not consumed for religious reasons.
Danielle, 19
– 11 years with a missionary organisation

66

I find the Aussie obsession with drinking (and gambling for that matter) to be an ugly side of the culture in this country. It's definitely not something I engage with, and my social/friendship circle is also largely removed from that side of life here."
Tamar, 50
– 18 years in the business sector

66

Australia's drinking culture is toxic. I don't engage with it anymore.
Shellie, 54
– 1 year with the ADF

66

Australia's drinking culture is hard core in places and more controlled in others. I visit pubs for a beer and drink at home.
Marco, 64
– 11 years with a missionary organisation, 5 years with the ADF

Although you must be 18 years old to legally drink, many minors under the age of 18 bring alcohol to their own parties, and some Australian parents procure alcohol for their children's parties. Under Australian law, a parent/guardian can give alcohol to their own child on private property – but not to other children, unless their parent/guardian has given consent.

If you return to Australia before the age of 18, it is important to be aware of this aspect of Australia's drinking culture beforehand. You may want to talk to parents and other trusted adults about their views on alcohol and what to do if you find yourself in an unsafe situation. For example, my (Tanya's) parents made it clear to me from an early age (around 12) that if I was ever in a situation that felt unsafe to me, or my only way home was with someone who had been drinking, I could call them at any time of night and they would pick me up.

University is a time when overuse of alcohol is more common, and in some groups there can be more peer pressure to join in. That said, Australia's drinking culture is changing over time. There is now less peer pressure than there once was, and the amount of underage drinking in Australia (especially binge drinking) is trending down. If you are concerned about pressure to drink, you may like to practise responses, but a simple "I don't feel like having a drink" or "I'm fine with Coke" is often enough.

"
I would say Australia's drinking culture can be really toxic at times but at the same time it does not push you into it if you do not want to be a part of it. I find that a lot of people are very understanding of my opinions of not wanting to drink as much as them, or at all. I only drink casually at some events, maybe once every six months.
Milly, 21
– 10 years for family reasons

"
The need to have a designated driver has taken some of the pressure to drink away. How strong the drinking culture is seems to vary a lot between different social circles.
Chris, 58
– 1 year in the business sector

Whatever age you are, you do not have to drink. Just because others are, and because you can, does not mean you have to. Most Australians now respect a no, or a slow, response to drinking alcohol – especially when there is a need for a designated driver. Some common non-alcoholic options for after-work drinks at the pub include soft drinks, juice, cordial syrups mixed with soda water, or the very common 'lemon, lime and bitters' (real bitters is alcoholic, but only a few drops are used). Some pubs/bars will now have a non-alcoholic beer or wine option. If you go to a nice bar with a cocktail menu, they will most likely have a range of mocktails – non-alcoholic cocktails – which are delicious alternatives. Most will also make 'virgin' (non-alcoholic) versions of their signature cocktails for you.

"
Among young people (uni age), there's pressure to drink from peers. Perhaps even more than that, a lot of young people don't really feel comfortable having a good time without alcohol on board. I was certainly seen as a bit weird for being a non-drinker. During uni I volunteered with Red Frogs* (providing assistance

to students at big party events), so I saw and looked after a lot of drunk students while I was sober. It definitely made alcohol seem even less attractive. On another level, I now need to engage with Australia's drinking culture as a doctor. Australian attitudes make it hard for people to recognise when alcohol is contributing to poor health and it's so hard to stop participating in drinking.
Katie, 24
– 14 years with a missionary organisation

"
Big drinking, big nights, are commonly accepted and assumed for young people. From age 30 onwards it definitely slows down to more relaxed drinks with friends around food, picnics, beach days, etc. Having a drink with someone is usually a gesture of warm friendship and acceptance. Work Christmas parties usually involve drinking and a few people getting drunk. I have enjoyed some fun nights of dancing and drinks with friends I know well and trust. More often, though, I enjoy a casual drink with friends or family over dinner or a social hangout.
Anna, 29
– 16 years with a missionary organisation

If you choose to drink, and you are also a driver, it is vital to be aware of the impact of alcohol on your ability to drive safely. Knowing how many standard drinks you are consuming and what approximate blood alcohol level that puts you at is an important skill to learn. The blood alcohol limit for drivers in Australia is 0.05, but for those with special licences it is zero. Special licences include: learners, provisional, probationary, taxi, public transit, and heavy vehicles.

When I (Tanya) was in Grades 7–8 in Australia, we had lessons on alcohol consumption in health class. We were taught what a standard drink was and how to calculate the amount of alcohol in different drinks. I have found this sort of basic knowledge of alcohol consumption rare in the TCK communities I have worked with. A great resource to improve your knowledge of how alcohol affects people, what a standard drink is, and why that matters, is the Australian Government Department of Health website: health.gov.au/health-topics/alcohol

Visiting

When Australians visit one another at home it is usually simply a chance for company and conversation, not a formal occasion. There are no special rituals to perform – no guest language, no guest gift, etc. The language used in an invitation to visit is generally casual; you will usually be invited to "come round and hang out" or "come over for a cuppa*". You may only be invited into one or two rooms of the house, and other doors may be closed, as this is a private area for them. Some friends may offer you a tour of their home, but not all will; this should not be expected or asked for.

It is important to plan ahead before visiting Australians at home. Often there will be days (even weeks!) between making a plan and the planned visit occurring. Even when visiting a close friend or neighbour you've visited many times, it is customary to call or text ahead of time to check if it is a convenient time for them. Do not show up without permission. It's also important to confirm who is coming with you – don't bring unplanned guests to your friend's home.

In the same way, if you would like people to visit your home, give them time to plan. Don't expect them to be available on short notice, but instead offer several times/dates to see what works with their schedule. Australians tend not to take short-notice invitations (less than a week's notice) too seriously, and it is not rude to decline such an invitation.

66
I usually go out with friends rather than to their houses but when I do it is usually arranged at a set time, often a casual occasion to catch up, play games, or cook. Every now and then there will be a birthday party.
Danielle, 19
– 11 years with a missionary organisation

> **"**
> *I visit my friends' houses on a regular basis. Sometimes I bring a gift or some food, sometimes I don't. Most of the time I bring board games, card games, and other things to do. Sometimes it is really spontaneous, sometimes we have planned it two weeks in advance.*
> Milly, 21
> – 10 years for family reasons

> **"**
> *I visit my sister and brother-in-law weekly. There's no arranged time, but I'll call before I go so they have time to prepare before I arrive. I like to bring a snack to share or a game to play. I can drop in on my grandparents any time without calling because they're more old school (they didn't have phones growing up). With my friends, we have an arranged time and date because we're all busy.*
> Opal, 28
> – 15 years with a missionary organisation

> **"**
> *I visit my friends' houses all the time. I have a small circle of very close friends that I enjoy spending time with. It's very informal, and we often bring something to share – some food, a bottle of wine, etc.*
> Tamar, 50
> – 18 years in the business sector

Avoid staying too long on a single visit; two hours would be considered enough time for most simple visits (parties and large gatherings often last much longer). Always leave before the next mealtime, unless you are specifically invited to stay on for the meal. If you do stay for a meal, offer to help clean up afterwards with your host. It is common in Australia for guests to help clear the table and clean dishes, especially if the hosts have done a lot of cooking or there is a lot of cleaning up to be done, but it is not required.

Meals at friends' homes

When you have been invited for a meal, contact the host to see if they would like you to bring something to contribute (this can be food or drink). If they say there is no need, it is fine to arrive empty handed.

(Neither guests nor hosts are expected to give gifts during/after visits.) If you would like to bring something, some small snacks to share before the meal or small sweet treats for after would be appropriate. Homemade or store bought are both fine. If you will be sharing a meal (and you know your hosts drink alcohol), a bottle of wine to share is another common contribution.

66
I am involved with the Persian community here (as my husband is Iranian), and with that culture we often visit homes and bring gifts. With my Aussie friends, we don't visit all that often and I would just bring chocolates.
Rebecca, 33
– 5 years with a missionary organisation

Your host will not be offended if you clean your plate, or if you leave a small amount behind – either is fine. You are welcome to accept second helpings of food you enjoyed, but this is not required. If you have had enough, simply say so – this is not rude. It is polite for your host to offer, but it is not rude for you to decline. If there is enough left for seconds, you may also ask for or even serve yourself some before they are offered – most hosts will be very happy to know you enjoyed the food enough to want more!

When you have finished your meal, place your knife and fork together on top of your plate. They don't have to be in a particular position, but straight up and down across the plate or turned slightly anticlockwise from there are common. If your knife and fork are separate on the plate (especially if they are not parallel), most people will assume you are still eating.

Meal times

There are a lot of different meals Australians can invite you to!

♦ Breakfast (brekky) is usually the first meal of the day.
♦ Brunch is a relaxed meal between breakfast and lunch, usually taking the place of both; it is commonly enjoyed on weekends or holidays.

- Morning Tea is a mid-morning snack. On a job site, this may be called 'smoko*' as it was when workers would take a cigarette (smoke) break.
- Lunch is a meal eaten in the middle of the day (sometimes called 'Dinner', especially if it is a heavy meal; more commonly used in rural areas) typically eaten around 12–1 pm.
- Afternoon Tea is a mid-afternoon snack, also known as 'smoko'.
- Dinner, also known as Tea, is a main evening meal typically eaten around 6–7 pm.
- Supper is a snack after dinner, before bedtime.

Barbecues

Australians are known for their barbecues (BBQs/barbies). Barbies are generally informal, outdoor meals, in which food is cooked on a BBQ/grill. When multiple people are invited it is often expected that the guest will bring something to share. This can include meat, salad, other side dishes, or bread. This practice is sometimes referred to as 'bringing a plate'. If you are asked to bring a plate and are unsure about what to bring, try writing to your host for a suggestion – would they like you to bring chips*, or a salad? You might suggest a side-dish you enjoy making to see if they think it is a good idea. Also, if a host says a party or gathering is BYO (Bring Your Own), this means they will not be providing alcoholic drinks, and guests should therefore bring their own. BYO is sometimes used in other contexts. For example: "BYO meat, everything else provided."

> **"**
> *Australian hosts can usually be taken at their word if they say not to bring anything, and will generally be happy to tell you if there is something they want you to bring. I very rarely bring gifts unless there's a birthday. I try to help clean up after a meal, but if I'm not quick enough the host does it before I get the chance. I would then dry the dishes if they're washing.*
> Katie, 24
> – 14 years with a missionary organisation

> **"**
> *Usually my visits to friends' houses are casual. It is polite to ask what you can bring if the visit involves a meal. Otherwise bringing*

a snack and/or drink (non-alcoholic) to share is appropriate regardless. If you know there will be social drinking then the appropriate thing to do is to bring alcoholic drinks for yourself and not expect others to share theirs necessarily, but often they will. It is then polite to share yours in return.
Anna, 29
– 16 years with a missionary organisation

Gifts

Australia does not have a strong gift-giving culture. Gifts are usually only exchanged on special occasions, such as birthdays and Christmas, or given to a person being honoured at a special event, such as a wedding, baby shower, graduation, or retirement party.

66
Australia doesn't have a gift-giving culture; Australians only give gifts for birthdays and Christmas. Where I live now people are always taking little things, mostly from the garden, to each other.
Marco, 64
– 11 years with a missionary organisation, 5 years with the ADF

Generally speaking, most Australians are not expecting gifts worth a fortune, but instead prefer gifts that reflect their interests and/or their friendship with the giver. A card is usually given along with the gift, and the giver will write a short message (one or two sentences) expressing their good wishes or appreciation for the recipient.

66
Gift exchanging is different in Australia than where I grew up. It is less carefully balanced in terms of value, and isn't really kept track of that closely. It would be considered a bit rude in Australia to give nothing or something very small after someone gave you something quite nice, but it's not all that closely compared.
Katie, 24
– 14 years with a missionary organisation

Gifts are usually opened when received, in front of the person giving the gift. This allows the recipient to express their gratitude directly to the gift-giver. In the case of a large event with a lot of gifts, there may be a time during the event for opening gifts, or the gifts may be opened after the event. In this case, thank-you cards will usually be sent.

"
Gifts aren't a big thing in Australia. Theoretically it's all very casual, but there are subtle conventions. If a person who won't be at a celebration on the day gives you a gift before your birthday, the custom is to ask if you can open it now (to show appreciation) and for the giver to say yes (to show it's no big deal). Then you admire whatever it is, and say thank you for the specific item. Also, you now have an onus to remember their birthday, and provide a gift of similar value.
Chris, 58
– 1 year in the business sector

Giving good gifts

1. **Go small**
   In most cases it's better to underdo it than overdo it. A lavish gift when others are giving small gifts (or no gifts) may be awkward. A small gift will still show thoughtfulness.

2. **Sentiment over splash**
   A gift that is meaningful to the person is always a good idea! Showing you know them by remembering their favourite snack, flower, author – or even giving a gift card for their favourite store – will be more meaningful than a big gift that doesn't connect to their interests.

3. **Ask!**
   It's okay to ask for suggestions! You can ask a mutual friend for ideas of what would be good, or just ask the person if there's anything they want/need.

4. **Team Up**
   Group gifts are okay as well! This lets you pool your money with other mutual friends to buy something bigger than any of you could afford alone.

Chapter 7:

Talking to Australians

Arrogance

Something we have said several times already (and will say several times more) is that Australians have a problem with arrogance. In Australia, arrogance is a cultural no-no.

> **"**
>   *Australians seem to be a pretty easy-going bunch, but there are some unwritten rules. You don't show off, and don't verbally express how well you have done something. This also might be tied to the trouble Australians have with accepting compliments, as it's a fine line between being polite and giving recognition to what the other party has expressed but not agreeing with it too much.*
> Claire, 27
> – 9 years with a missionary organisation

There is a lot of cultural baggage embedded in this. Mainstream Anglo culture descends from people rejected by Britain. Whether they were transported as petty criminals or political dissidents (with no way to return home), third or fourth sons of 'noble' families with no prospects, or the type who sought adventure and a new life because they didn't fit in, many of the Anglos who began colonial culture in Australia left the highly structured social classes of Britain. To this was added wave after wave of immigrants and refugees seeking a new life with opportunities – whether coming during the gold rushes, fleeing war in their homelands, seeking greater opportunities, or rejecting the norms of the lands in which they were born.

Over time, this has morphed into an Australian cultural norm that is offended by people placing themselves above others – or appearing to, as judged by an Australian audience. Anything that makes you appear arrogant (such as listing your accomplishments during introductions, for example) will alienate you from potential friends. In fact, the anti-American sentiment common in Australia is often a reaction to misreading American cultural norms as arrogance. Even accepting compliments too readily can be read as arrogance by some Australians.

> **66**
> *I've definitely seen anti-American sentiment among Australians. We have a love-hate relationship with the US. Maybe it's the same way New Zealand has a love-hate of Australia, the domineering big brother.*
> Marco, 64
> – 11 years with a missionary organisation, 5 years with the ADF

> **66**
> *I don't like it when people generalise about America or Americans – I know so many very different and lovely Americans, and the country is diverse.*
> Shellie, 54
> – 1 year with the ADF

The Australian horror of arrogance is written into our language. 'Tall poppy syndrome*' describes the Australian propensity to tear down anyone who dares to shine. To be 'up oneself*' is a common insult, describing a person who thinks too much of themselves, or is self-absorbed. It is a crucial part of Australian humour as well, which we will share in a section dedicated to that topic.

Understanding this unspoken rule – that arrogance is wrong – is crucial to understanding how Australians act and interact. No one raised in Australian culture can see this clearly. It took me (Tanya) many years of living outside Australia to begin to unpack it. For Australian TCKs who were not raised in Australia, these sorts of unwritten rules can be jarring and even hurtful. 'Culture' is not an excuse to be hurtful to others, but recognising cultural norms at work can help us see intent more clearly, and have fruitful conversations about impact.

For now, here are some tips to get you started in unpacking Australia's anti-arrogance culture:

1. **Embrace humility**
   Lean into the Australian value of humility. See the value in not praising yourself, not looking for what makes one person

rank higher than another. Australians don't do this perfectly by any means, but there is a positive value here worth embracing.

2. Compliment others

Australians are often terrible at accepting genuine compliments, which can go beyond humility into a sense of humiliation. Bucking that trend by saying kind things to the people in your life may make them uncomfortable at first, but it's a good thing to get comfortable with!

3. Ask them about their life

One of the fastest ways to break through the bluster of anti-arrogance, no-tall-poppies Australians is to ask about their lives. To learn about their families, their favourite things, what they enjoy doing – and show genuine interest. Often you'll find something in common! Even if you don't, most people soften when they share about the things that bring them joy. Even if that's explaining the meaning behind their tattoos!

Language

Australians are passionate about their language – both the accent and the dialect itself. In 'Australian Voices' on the Macquarie University website, Professor Felicity Cox and Dr Sallyanne Palethorpe write: "Australian English functions as a significant and extremely powerful symbol of national identity. It is one of the well-known World Englishes and is a mature dialect with its own internal norms and standards." (Cox, F. and Palethorpe, S. (2010) *Australian Voices*, Macquarie University, Australian Voices).

"G'day* mate" is one of the most well-known Australian sayings, but Australians also use a whole lot of unusual slang in everyday life. When I (Kath) first moved overseas, I had to explain myself a lot as I would use slang words I just assumed everyone understood. I learned to say I was wearing my flip-flops instead of my thongs*, for example! I (Tanya) have switched between Australian-dominant and American-dominant

English-speaking worlds so many times, my brain often stalls trying to remember which words to use where – sometimes in my own home!

Australians often shorten words. A cup of tea/coffee is a *cuppa*, a sandwich is a *sanga*, McDonald's is *maccas*, breakfast is *brekky*, sunglasses are *sunnies*, mosquito is *mozzie*, tradesman (contractor) is *tradie*, present is *pressie*, football is *footy*, relatives are *rellies* or *relos*, devastated is *devo*, garbage collector is *garbo*, conversation is *convo*, combination is *combo*, aggressive is *aggro*, avocado is *avo*, afternoon is *arvo*, and cabernet sauvignon is *cab sav*. And the list goes on, and on, and on.

> **"**
> *There are so many different accents, across states or even within a state, which is interesting. Some are quite subtle and don't seem too distinguishable as Australian but others are very Australian. Oftentimes, it's the Aussie slang that makes the accent more Australian.*
> Danielle, 19
> – 11 years with a missionary organisation

> **"**
> *When you first come back, the Aussie accent hits you like a brick. I've been back long enough that it's back to normal now, but boy, that twang stands out in a crowd overseas.*
> Derek, 45
> – 10 years with a missionary organisation

People newly arrived in Australia have no clue what is being said half the time. Even within Australia the slang and vocabulary change from state to state. For example, what we call *fritz** in South Australia (where Kath grew up) is known as *devon** in NSW (where Tanya grew up) and *polony* in WA. (If you grew up in the USA or with Americans, you might know it as *bologna* instead.) Another one is the name for what you wear when going swimming – is it *bathers, cossie, swimmers, swimsuit,* or *togs*? And don't get us started on the great *potato scallop**/*potato cake** (or apparently *potato fritter*) debate! That's an easy way to get Aussies fired up. Check out our glossary in the *Resources* section for all the Australian words used in this book, along with some more of our favourite Australian slang.

Swearing

Australians overseas are often known for their swearing. That's largely because Australian perceptions of swearing – what it is and when it is rude – differ from other cultures, including other English-speaking cultures. In addition, swearing is censored less heavily in Australian media. About the only swear word regularly bleeped on prime-time television in Australia is the F-bomb, and even that goes out freely outside prime time and on the play-on-demand apps and paid services.

66
Swearing in Australia is very excessive but there was also lots of swearing overseas.
Olivia, 23
– 10 years with a missionary organisation

66
Compared to Americans I feel like we swear a lot. Our Australian humour also includes lots of coarse jokes. Mambo t-shirts of yesteryear were a shock when I first saw them.*
Johnny, 36
– 18 years for family reasons

66
I do think that Australians swear a lot. It always took time to get used to on my return to Australia.
Marco, 64
– 11 years with a missionary organisation, 5 years with the ADF

Understanding Australian swearing

In Australia, intent is considered offensive more than the specific word used. Australians generally put swear words into three categories of use. The same swear word is received differently depending on its usage, and the intent behind its use.

1. **Outbursts**
   This is for when you are surprised – perhaps you hit your thumb with a hammer, for example – and react instinctively with a swear word: "Oh sh**!" This category of swearing is not offensive to the vast majority of Australians.

2. **Emphasis**
   Sometimes you need something stronger than very, or extremely – so you use a swear adjective to express just how strongly you feel. For example: "This has been a sh**ty week." Again, this category of words is not offensive to most Australians.

3. **Swearing *at* another person**
   Here, intent is key. Australian friends may swear at each other in an affectionate way – something incomprehensible to some cultures. Yet the exact same phrase will be extremely offensive when said to a stranger, or with a different tone of voice. For example, my (Tanya's) sister might tell me to f*** off in a playful way – which would not be offensive at all. If a stranger yelled that at me, it would of course be very offensive! Rule of thumb: if an Australian is smiling, their swearing is not intended to be offensive. If they don't know you, are looking at you, directing their comment to you, and aren't smiling – that's when it's probably intended to cause offence.

"
Swearing in Australia is totally normal and comfortable.
Christina, 59
– 13 years in the business sector

"
Everyday Aussie talk has many words that are considered swearing in many circles!
Brush, 70
– 12 years with a missionary organisation

As with Australian drinking culture, Australia's swearing culture is totally optional. You don't have to swear just because other Aussies do! In fact, you should be careful not to unless (until) you're sure you're clear on the rules of use in the particular group you're in – some communities are more swear-forward than others. The important thing to keep in mind is that swearing in Australia is often very casual, usually friendly, and not intended to upset you or make you feel uncomfortable.

> **"**
> *Swearing is normalised here A LOT. It has become comfortable for me to hear after returning to Australia as it's not acceptable in our overseas country amongst the expat community. I still don't swear myself.*
> Rebecca, 33
> – 5 years with a missionary organisation

Humour

The Australian sense of humour is a bit different to what you find in most other English-speaking countries. There is a lot of sarcasm, a lot of self-deprecation and making fun of others, and a good dose of swearing (see above). Add in Australian slang and a laidback style of storytelling and it really can be a bit incomprehensible at first!

> **"**
> *Australian humour is often light-hearted but can put others or themselves down. Self-deprecating humour has become more frequent. Most of the time it is harmless and I have participated in it; however, it can quickly stop being humorous.*
> Danielle, 19
> – 11 years with a missionary organisation

> **"**
> *It is fascinating that Aussie humour is different to most places. I often sat in movies and laughed at very different times to the rest of the crowds.*
> Brush, 70
> – 12 years with a missionary organisation

Deadpan humour

Part of what can be tricky about Australian humour is that it is 'high context' and played straight – something known colloquially as 'deadpan*' humour. 'High context' means that much of the time, there is a lot you need to know in order to get the joke. 'Callbacks' – where a joke plays on something said earlier – are considered particularly funny.

But riffing on what's happening in current events and pop culture, and referring to events and pop culture of previous decades, is also common. This makes Australian humour somewhat inaccessible for people who are new to the culture – including some Australians!

Deadpan* humour involves saying humorous things with a straight face, no smile, and no laugh. The audience (whether those watching a stand-up comic, or a few friends gathered) know to laugh from the 'high context' clues alone. My (Tanya's) grandfather was such a master of deadpan humour that sometimes his own children/grandchildren were uncertain if he was kidding or serious – until he gave a sly wink!

> **"**
> *Australian humour is high-context, dry, and witty. It relies heavily on shared context, by referencing previous parts of a conversation or shared cultural experiences. It also requires a level of cleverness to make puns or utilise sarcasm. Part of the humour is that you don't call attention to it, so it's weird to highlight or point out a joke. It's understated. In comparison, I find Canadian (and North American) humour loud, in your face, boring, and sometimes obnoxious. My sense of humour is VERY Australian. One of my closest Australian friends in Canada will have me in stitches in just about every conversation because our sense of humour is so similar. His dry commentary won't always seem like a joke to other people at the table, but I'll be doubled over laughing.*
> Lyndall, 30
> – 5 years for family reasons

Teasing

If someone in Australia teases you, it's a good idea to reply with a smile and show that you are not disconcerted by it. Indulging in jokes like this shows that you are self-confident but do not take yourself too seriously. Lightly teasing them back will also be received cheerfully. You may feel that making fun of you like this is rude, but it is a cultural practice that makes sense in context.

66

Growing up in another culture means I don't like the way some parts of Australian culture are about sarcasm and ribbing people. I find myself feeling offended on other people's behalf and feeling uncomfortable. I don't 'get' the joke.
Alice, 52
– 8 years with DFAT

66

I find it hard to really tease others the way Australian friends do."
Marco, 64
– 11 years with a missionary organisation, 5 years with the ADF

The teasing humour in Australian friendship is part of the culture's anti-arrogance value. Self-deprecating humour shows I am not arrogant – that I don't think too much of myself. Teasing friends shows I know they are not arrogant – that they don't think too much of themselves.

66

Australian humour is absolutely self-deprecating, teasing and bagging out* others or yourself – 100% tall poppy syndrome. I do use this humour a little but much less than my Australian friends, I feel, as I think some of it is rude and hurtful!
Rebecca, 33
– 5 years with a missionary organisation

Australians tend to tease or make fun of ('bag out*') their close friends and family even more than they would strangers or less close acquaintances. This is because the teasing is a way of showing that I know you do not see yourself as arrogant – high praise in Australia. It also means that Australians who are not aware of this dynamic can easily offend their non-Australian friends as they become closer and naturally begin teasing them. I (Tanya) found this out the hard way when one friend spoke to another asking if I'd said anything about having a problem with her: "I thought we were friends but she's been so mean to me lately!"

66

Australian humour is sarcastic and crude. I learnt it from my guy friends. It was funny while I was young and helped me to relate to them, until I realised it's hurtful. The humour is mean

and sometimes takes a dig at someone's dignity. This doesn't translate well for foreigners to Australia.
Opal, 28
– 15 years with a missionary organisation

"
I know I'm fairly sarcastic but sometimes it's too much. I don't understand always bagging each other out* in friendship. I'm too sensitive for that.
Jean, 33
– 18 years with a missionary organisation

One advantage of having lived outside Australia is the ability to critique our own culture. I (Tanya) spent years defending the Australian cultural practice of teasing friends as a form of affection. Eventually I was able to stand back and recognise that perhaps making fun of people isn't the best way to build friendship and show affection. You can recognise the intent behind the teasing without joining in, and if you don't enjoy it, you don't have to accept it.

"
Teasing seems to be a big part of friendships and to an extent it is all in good fun. However, from my perspective as a sensitive person, I don't appreciate it as much as some friends do and I myself don't often tease others. Perhaps this is part of the difficulty in making friends; if they feel you can't match their humour or banter, they don't have as much interest.
Danielle, 19
– 11 years with a missionary organisation

So yes, Australians like to 'take the piss*' out of each other, which often includes making jokes about someone to their face. Please note, however, that making the same joke about someone when they are not present is usually the sign of a nasty person, not a friend. And in either case, you do not have to participate if it makes you uncomfortable.

Small talk

When I (Kath) was living in Cambodia, a Cambodian colleague at the international school asked me about appropriate small talk in Australia.

Whenever our boss returned from an overseas trip, she would tell him, "Oh, you're bigger!" which shocked people. I explained to her that in Australia we don't often talk about weight – this is considered somewhat taboo. In much of Asia it is quite normal to ask a person's age or marital status when first meeting. In Australia this is considered too direct and personal. Other topics considered off-limits in Australian small talk include salary, parents' occupation, and religion.

> **"**
> *The basic questions Nepali people ask are: What's your name? How old are you? Are you married? What religion are you? Many Australians would not want to talk about this in their first conversation, but it's very common in Nepal even with someone you don't know.*
> Georgia, 38
> – 9 years with a missionary organisation

So, what *is* it normal to talk about in Australia? Common small talk topics include: the weather, plans for the weekend, news/current events, sport, movies/TV shows, local events, restaurants, and pets. These can be great topics to start or continue a conversation with someone you don't know well. This will help you get to know a person without getting too personal and making them feel uncomfortable. Here are some suggestions from Aussie TCKs:

> **"**
> *Small talk in Australia is about sport, TV shows, and movies.*
> Derek, 45
> – 10 years with a missionary organisation

> **"**
> *It looks like jokes, jibes, 'How was your week?', bagging out* the government/systems, and relaxed conversation.*
> Rebecca, 33
> – 5 years with a missionary organisation

> **"**
> *It's footy (I hate footy), what you're watching on Netflix, how cute your nephews and nieces are, the funny thing your dog did.*
> Opal, 28
> – 15 years with a missionary organisation

> **"**
> *You ask what subjects you're doing at school, or what you're studying at uni. Or you talk about how Melbourne weather is absolute chaos.*
> Amelie, 18
> – 10 years with a missionary organisation

Good questions to get a conversation started – leaving it open for them to select a topic – include:

- ♦ "How's your day going?" or simply "How are you going?*"
- ♦ "Did you have a good week?"
- ♦ "What are you up to this weekend?"
- ♦ "What have you been watching/reading/listening to lately?"

Sport

Sport is a huge part of the Australian consciousness. It takes up a lot of space physically (with lots of space given to courts/ovals, etc.) and mentally/emotionally (it's talked about, played, and cared about by many people around the country). The reason we have included sport in our conversation section is that knowing a bit about popular Australian sports will get you a long way in Australian small talk. For Australian TCKs, however, it often feels very difficult to join in.

> **"**
> *I find the Australian sport obsession pointless and childish, but I conceal it – I've come to recognise talking about sport is a way people seek to engage with each other, and it's polite to go along with it. I track sport just enough to be a good listener.*
> Chris, 58
> – 1 year in the business sector

> **"**
> *I think Australia's sport obsession is weird. I don't enjoy watching AFL, rugby, or cricket, which are the typical Australian sports. So this does not help me connect with others.*
> Milly, 21
> – 10 years for family reasons

> *I watch a bit of AFL, though otherwise I'm not very engaged with sport, but it definitely is a big social aspect in many people's lives. I used to do Parkrun every Saturday morning – a lot of people find it motivating to run each week with others.*
Danielle, 19
– 11 years with a missionary organisation

I (Kath) tried my hand at netball and basketball as a young person, then settled on touch football. I don't play a sport anymore but I do watch it. I enjoy being a spectator in a crowd even when I don't understand the rules. I (Tanya) played netball and backyard cricket growing up, and watched a lot of rugby league – on TV and in person. The rest of my family are sportier than me – between them, my parents and sisters have played netball, cricket, tennis, soccer, rugby league, touch football, jiujitsu, and ultimate frisbee.

While it's always completely okay to opt out of an activity/interest you don't enjoy, given how big sport is in Australia, we want to use this section to give you a quick primer on Australian sport – to help you understand some basics and first steps if you want to test the waters and try joining in.

> *I do not play sport, which is one of the big things that I missed out on by being overseas as a kid. Sport does not interest me much, which often leaves me out of all the talk going on around me. I feel like a 'bad Australian' when footy talk starts or at finals time.*
Brush, 70
– 12 years with a missionary organisation

> *Living outside Australia meant missing out on the sport culture, which is a big way for men to relate to each other.*
Dayong, 29
– 7 years with a missionary organisation

THONGS OR FLIP-FLOPS? 👣

> **"**
> *Sport isn't a part of my life. I don't really understand Australian sports (cricket, footy, etc.). Sometimes people are almost offended when I say I don't understand these sports or follow a team. Fortunately, saying I grew up in the wrong country usually satisfies them.*
> Amelie, 18
> – 10 years with a missionary organisation

Football in Australia

When it comes to football (or footy), Australia has four 'codes' – a term used to group four sports all labelled types of 'football' in Australia:

1. Australian Football, also known as Aussie Rules (AFL, Australian Football League)
2. Rugby League (NRL, National Rugby League)
3. Rugby Union (Super Rugby)
4. Soccer (A-League)

Yes, in Australia we call it soccer – to separate it from all the other sports we also call football! There is even an increasing number of people who watch American football (NFL, also known in Australia as gridiron), although it is rarely played here.

Most of the top football competitions in Australia include teams from New Zealand. The Super Rugby competition also includes teams from Pacific Island nations.

Different codes are more dominant in different states, and different areas within states. If Aussie rules is dominant in your area, then that's probably what 'footy' will mean there. If rugby league is dominant, then 'footy' will probably refer to rugby league instead. There are also big rivalries between different states – such as the rugby league State of Origin tournament between NSW and QLD. It was a bit unusual for me (Kath) to play touch football, for example, as it is associated with rugby league, and therefore NSW, not SA (where I live) – but my dad grew up in NSW so we all grew up watching rugby league.

❝
I hate sport, so that was definitely tricky for me, especially before my gender transition. 'What team do you go for?' is one of the biggest questions you get asked as a guy. I was like, I don't know, I hate sport – it's just a whole heap of people like bumping into each other.*
Cardamon, 23
– 11 years in aid and development

Cricket

Cricket is another huge passion in Australia, especially during the summer months. Many people who grew up in Australia in the 70s, 80s, and 90s knew the voice of legendary cricket commentator Richie Benaud as 'the sound of summer' because the cricket was always on in the background – even if you weren't actually paying attention.

There are three main forms of the game:

1. **Test Cricket**
   Test cricket is the oldest form and is considered the most prestigious to play. Players wear all white, and a single match can last up to four or five days. Each team bats until every player gets out or the batting side 'declares', indicating that they think they have scored enough runs to win. Australia players wear dark green caps called "the baggy green" which are a symbol of being in the Test team.

2. **One Day**
   ODI cricket (One Day Internationals, known as 'one dayers') has been around since the 1970s. These matches last for one day with limited playing time for each side, and the players wear colourful outfits.

3. **T20**
   T20 is the newest and shortest form of the game and is the best introduction if you are new to cricket. The domestic Australian T20 competition is called the Big Bash League (BBL). Tickets are cheap, matches are usually played in the late afternoon/evening or on weekends, and there is lots of colour, noise, and atmosphere.

66
Australia certainly does love its sport, but I don't have any particularly strong feelings about it. I enjoy cricket well enough and I'm happy to watch it, but don't usually bother following it closely except to engage with friends who are really into it.
Katie, 24
– 14 years with a missionary organisation

Connecting through sport

Playing sports is a great way to make friends in Australia. Many teams meet for practice at least once a week in addition to playing competitively once a week, so you have lots of time around the same group of people who share something in common. Adult sport is huge in Australia – no matter where you live, there will be a selection of team sports to join, and probably some martial arts clubs and other social sporting activities as well. There are almost always teams for novice players who want to exercise and make friends more than compete.

66
Playing sport has provided connection for me in Australia, but not spectator sport, which is an obsession for some.
Rho, 60+
– 2 years in aid and development

66
Sport was a key way to connect in adjusting back to Australian life and often a point of connection in building bridges with people both in Australia and beyond.
David, 61
– 6 years in aid and development

If you are at a loss on how to connect with people at school or work, find out what sport they follow and learn a little! It is an investment, but you gain a way into a lot of conversations. If sport is something you already enjoy, why not invest in learning a new sport that will help you connect and make friends? I (Tanya) resisted learning a new sport overseas that many of my friends enjoyed for years. When I finally decided to join in, I realised my pride had robbed me of years of fun.

Getting started with Australian sport

1. **Learn the rules**

   Sport is more fun to watch when you understand what's happening. If you learn best by reading, look up the rules online – perhaps use a 'for dummies' search term to make sure you get easy-entry rules to get started with! Otherwise – or in addition – ask friends to teach you. This can be a great way to build a friendship as well as gain a hobby.

2. **Pick a team**

   Another thing that makes sport fun is having a team to cheer for, and other fans to celebrate (or commiserate) with. You might simply choose the local team where you live, or maybe there is another part of the country that is also 'home' which you'd like to feel connected to, or you could join a friend and cheer for their favourite team. Usually, Australians simply say 'go for' or perhaps 'barrack for' a team. Definitely do not use the American phrase 'root for' a team in Australia. In Australia the word 'root' is slang for 'have sex with' so won't come across quite the way you intended!

3. **Watch**

   There are lots of ways to watch Australian sport, including lots of online options. The five free-to-air channels (ABC, SBS, Channel 7, Channel 9, and Channel 10) all have online streaming available for free within Australia, and this includes a lot of sport. When you watch televised sport, the commentary often tells you a lot about what is going on, which can help you better understand.

4. **Go to a live game**

   Any time you get a chance, we really recommend that you go to a live game of whatever sport is big where you are. You will see what we mean when we say Australians are passionate about their sport! But even local matches are fun. If a friend of yours plays in a competitive league, go watch them play sometime and cheer for them. It can be a bit of fun and a way to build relationships.

❝
My housemate taught me the rules of NRL a bit (with difficulty) so I could understand what was going on. When she's around I follow her team closely enough to follow what she says about it, but I don't enjoy watching or following it without her.
Katie, 24
– 14 years with a missionary organisation

❝
I think sport is a good way to connect with people. My workplace has a social netball team but even that seems quite competitive and I haven't joined because I haven't learned netball! Instead, my husband and I often use our bushwalks and hikes as ways to invite others to join us and allow conversation to flow and connection and relationships to grow.
Anna, 29
– 16 years with a missionary organisation

Reality TV

Reality TV has a prominent place on Australian television screens. There is actually a policy reason behind this. The government requires that 55% of all content shown on Australia's free-to-air channels be Australian. Reality TV is an easy way to do this, so Australian reality TV shows are often much longer – both longer episodes and more episodes per season – than their international counterparts.

For example, while a US season of *MasterChef* may have 20 episodes, an Australian season might have 60 episodes – or more – airing five nights a week for three months. *Australian Survivor* airs not once but three nights per week, with the contestants spending up to 30% longer in the wilderness (50 days vs 39 days maximum). All the reality TV shows are also endlessly promoted in the lead-up to their season premiere, and throughout their run.

Lots of Australians are addicted to reality television, but even among casual watchers it's easy for these shows to sink into general discourse. Sometimes these discussions even make their way into the news because they are part of public consciousness.

> *I haven't watched much (or any) Australian TV since I've come back to Australia, but I do know of the reality TV shows that people are watching. A lot of people are interested in Married At First Sight as well as The Block.*
Milly, 21
– 10 years for family reasons

> *It's hard not to get sucked into some Australian reality TV shows! And definitely, it can be something fun to chat about with friends – even my kids!*
Tamar, 50
– 18 years in the business sector

Watching Australian reality TV is also an easy way to start preparing for repatriation. Reality TV showcases different types of Australian accents, the contestants tend to use a lot of slang, and they often talk about Australian people and places that offer background knowledge which can prove useful later on. Watching Australian *MasterChef* while living in China with my (Tanya's) American husband led to several conversations about slang terms he assumed were individual quirks rather than common Australian terms I use myself while in Australia!

Pop culture knowledge

Pop culture is anything that looms large in public discourse. Sport and reality TV are two examples of 'pop culture' in Australia; we just explored why knowing about them helps us connect and engage in small talk. Common pop culture topics change depending on your age and where in Australia you live. Different local areas (and different sub-groups) will have their own specific pop culture topics.

> *People do like to talk about television especially; after joining Netflix I am a bit more engaged with pop culture. It's hard to avoid the big music hits everyone listens to but I don't engage with particular artists more than others so I wouldn't be able to talk more niche.*
Danielle, 19
– 11 years with a missionary organisation

> **"**
> *When it comes to pop culture, my friends and I usually talk about what's on Netflix, or an animated film, or anime. Anything in film or cartoons is within my interest. Lately, I've been looking for friends who are interested in K-pop. Because a lot of my classmates are Asian or foreign to Australia, I'm able to find friends who grew up watching and listening to the same things I did outside of Australia.*
> Opal, 28
> – 15 years with a missionary organisation

One way to get ideas for things to watch or listen to that might help you chat with others is to look for trending charts in Australia. What songs, shows, and movies are most watched, streamed, and purchased in Australia? If there's a specific genre you are personally into, look at the lists for that. Often you can even find breakdowns by age group to see what is popular among Australians of your age.

> **"**
> *I engage with all sorts of pop culture in Australia – music, movies, TV. I engage quite a lot with Australian radio and cinema.*
> Rebecca, 33
> – 5 years with a missionary organisation

Triple J is a national youth-focused radio station which also has an important role in unearthing new Australian music, with a quota of 40% Australian content (compared to 25% on commercial channels). It is a go-to station for many listeners under 40. The Triple J "hottest one hundred" has been a cultural touchpoint for decades. Near the end of January, usually on a public holiday or weekend, Triple J hosts a countdown of the top 100 songs released in the previous year as voted for in advance by listeners. It is common for people to host listening parties to enjoy the music. Playlists of previous countdowns can be a good way to learn songs many Australians have enjoyed each year.

As with sport, while pop culture can be an easy way into conversation, it's not a requirement. You can opt out and find different ways to engage.

"

People often chat about what they're watching on Netflix and ask what I'm watching. Live music festivals and gigs are a big deal here too. But the arts and pop culture scene is so diverse and I find I don't need to be involved in it to be friends. I've always been okay with saying 'I haven't seen that' or 'We don't have a TV'. Other ways I can redirect is to say, 'Oh that's interesting, but probably not my thing,' or, 'I like these kinds of artists or music,' to introduce my own interests.

Anna, 29
– 16 years with a missionary organisation

Section 3:
Being an Australian Adult, Anywhere in the World

Chapter 8:

Official Australian Documents

Being a citizen of a country – any country – comes with both rights and responsibilities. Every country has its own bureaucracy for navigating those rights and responsibilities. Even Australians who grew up in Australia their whole lives sometimes struggle with navigating Australian government services, required forms, and all the other life administration that comes with being an adult.

TCKs often find navigating these processes especially stressful. They may feel foreign to you – or make you feel foreign in your own passport country. You might not even know that there are services available to you, or requirements you must fulfill, as an Australian citizen. Your parent/s may or may not be able to help you much either, given that they may have spent a lot of time outside Australia too.

Common document struggles

Sorting out documents can be complicated and time-consuming. There are four main hurdles for TCKs trying to sort out their documents.

1. **Context**
    We have less context – we are less likely to understand the whats and whys because we have spent less time in the country. We may be missing certain experiences, have less information, or not understand certain terminology considered common knowledge by most Australians.

    66
    Some documents don't like to take into account that some of your key life points may not have taken place in Australia, and there is very little care from officials about it.
    Tayo, 21
    – 6 years with the ADF

2. **Expectations**
    Our lives don't always fit the expectations of those who create the

documents, or the forms that go with them. Your overseas addresses might not physically fit on forms. Your overseas documents may not be recognised. Almost half of our cohort said their lives didn't fit the boxes for some or many of the official documents they needed to fill in.

"
The main frustration for me is having to write down all the times you have ever lived overseas, including all the exact dates of leaving and returning. I'm sure I've never written them down the same way twice!
Matthew, 35
– 9 years with a missionary organisation

"
Completing past addresses and schooling on official documents was very daunting.
Jesse, 38
– 3 years with a missionary organisation

3. **Missing Documents**
Being born or educated outside Australia may mean you didn't naturally acquire (or even qualify for) documents considered standard in Australia.

"
There are many people born in Australian territories which have since attained independence who have significant issues applying for passports and other official documents because the current systems don't acknowledge their birth certificates as being Australian. It's an ongoing situation that causes significant stress.
Jane, 48
– 5 years in aid and development

4. **Inadequate support**
If you did not do high school in Australia, you probably had no access to guidance counsellors or social services with knowledge of the Australian system. The government-provided FAQs and helplines designed to provide assistance

(which we will list throughout this section and in the *Resources* section at the end of the book) often do not have clear answers to TCK dilemmas. One in five members of our cohort didn't have enough help navigating this area of life; one in four said it was very daunting and one in five said it caused them great anxiety. Less than a third of our cohort had no problems navigating official documents in Australia.

66

I would often try calling helplines when trying to complete official documents, but they never really understood my difficulties, let alone being able to actually help me figure them out.
Wren, 20
– 18 years with a missionary organisation

66

Accessing services is trickier than expected and sometimes it's hard to get the information you need to access them.
Jewel, 51
– 8 years with a missionary organisation

Australian documents for dummies

66

They're so confusing. I wish we had an 'Australian Documents for Dummies' book!
Zara, 19
– 5 years with a missionary organisation

It is because of such complications and concerns that we have written this section. In the next five chapters we break down the rights and responsibilities of holding Australian citizenship as an adult. This includes official documents, taxes, voting, resources, and services. We talk about what they are, why they matter, how to get/renew documents and access services, and whether you even need to. But first, here are some quick tips to get you started!

Quick tips for accessing services as a TCK

1. **Find a battle buddy**

    Get someone else involved to help fight the paperwork battle with you. Someone who is less emotionally invested (whose whole life does not depend on getting this paperwork sorted) can be a calm head, give good advice, remember things, and encourage you.

    "

    Getting either a social worker or asking a friend to help you can really be great. Having a social worker help me with government stuff was amazing; it was really helpful to have someone literally doing the parent stuff for you when you don't have that. It's stuff that you would go to your parents for help with, but my mum and dad don't know Australia, the ins and outs of Centrelink and myGov accounts and that stuff. And so you go to a social worker.
    Cardamon, 23
    – 11 years in aid and development

2. **Stay calm**

    It may be the twentieth (or hundredth) time you've tried to resolve the same issue, and you keep being told different things, and it's incredibly frustrating. Most of the time, however, the person you're talking to is encountering your type of situation for the first time. They probably have only been equipped with information pertaining to simple situations and know less about it than you do – but that isn't their fault. The system is making both of your lives difficult. They might even make a great battle buddy!

3. **Ask for a supervisor**

    Something I (Tanya) have learned is that while the first line of assistance will not know the answers, someone further down the line *can* help. I've found that "Do you have a supervisor who might have a suggestion for resolving this situation?" is a good line to have in your pocket. Let them know you don't expect them to have all the answers.

4. Get documents notarised ahead of time

If you have documents from overseas, get them authenticated (and translated if necessary) before you need to present them to be sighted by a local Australian authority. This saves time when they don't recognise (literally haven't seen before) your type of document.

Notarisation

Notarisation is a way to authenticate a document, or a copy of a document, through examination of the original. Depending on the kind of authentication you need, and what kind of document, there are lots of different ways to get it notarised. The most common is notary public services by a Justice of the Peace (JP).

It is helpful to learn the rules for document notarisation – and the different levels – and to get multiple notarised translations of any important documents that are written in other languages. For more information about notary services (both notary public, and document legalisation by DFAT), visit smartraveller.gov.au/consular-services/notarial-services

"

I have had great difficulty applying for official documents. When I applied for my Indian Overseas Citizenship, I needed my Brazilian birth certificate and its translation to be officially apostilled by DFAT in Canberra to be accepted by the Indian Embassy. Having multiple official documents (such as my birth certificate) not in English has caused difficulties and added paperwork applying for official documents here in Australia.
Nathan, 28
– 5 years with a missionary organisation

Points of Identification

'Points of Identification' is a system the Australian Government uses to combat identity theft by assigning a 'point value' to various documents according to how secure they are. To apply for most of the documents and benefits mentioned in this chapter, you will be required to prove your identity by providing documents up to a certain number of 'points' according to a scale provided to you. The more secure a document is, the more points it is worth. If you don't have highly secure documents establishing your identity, you will need a greater number of documents. The documents accepted, and the number of points assigned to each document, will be different for each issuing authority, so you'll need to check the website of the authority in question for precise details.

It is typical to be asked for 100 points of identity. You might only need to show two documents, depending on what you have. A passport, birth certificate, or citizenship certificate is typically worth 70 points, and a driver's licence or other government photo ID (including a university student ID) is typically worth 40 points. Lower security documents (worth only 20 points) might include a Medicare card, credit card, bank statement with transactions, Australian marriage certificate, or a current utility bill with your name and address on it.

Passports

In 2019–2020, 1.7 million Australian passports were issued, with 70% processed using online services. These 'online' services still require a visit to the local post office, but no appointment at a government office. The adult passport renewal service is quite simple to use, and usually works as planned without a hitch. Your passport application must be lodged at a participating Australia Post office, where they check your documents, you pay the fee, and they post the application packet to the passport office. It is common to arrange to have it returned to you by mail. When overseas, passport applications can be submitted at an Australian embassy or consulate (more on this in *Chapter 11*). For more information about your Australian passport, go to: passports.gov.au

66
I went to the post office alone to renew my passport. I don't remember it being that difficult.
Opal, 28
– 15 years with a missionary organisation

Expect to wait at least several weeks, and possibly several months, for your passport application to be processed. There is a rush service available, but it is much more expensive. A typical 10-year adult passport costs around $300; using the rush service nearly doubles that fee.

If your passport has expired, rather than renewing your valid passport you must apply for a new passport – a more difficult and complex process. More documentation must be presented, and a longer form filled out. Also, when you progress from a child's passport (issued to citizens under the age of 18 and valid for only five years) to an adult passport (10-year validity), the longer renewal process applies. (These processes are more complicated when conducted outside Australia as you must attend the embassy in person – see *Chapter 11* for more.)

> **"**
> *I recently got my first Australian adult passport. I was pleasantly surprised when I got it back in a few weeks. I had to fully reapply this time rather than renew my previous child passport. We expected it to be a much harder process than it was. As an Australian citizen I had access to necessary documents easily and only had to bring four with me. Some of the referee portions of the application were a little tricky to organise, but overall it was fairly smooth.*
> Danielle, 19
> – 11 years with a missionary organisation

A passport is almost essential while living outside Australia, but when you live in Australia it really isn't that important. Nearly half of Australians do not have a current valid passport – compared to only 10% of our cohort. Australian passports are rarely used for identification purposes within Australia. That said, if you have any intention of travelling overseas in the semi-near future, maintaining a valid passport is helpful. It is much easier to renew an existing passport than to apply for a new one once yours expires.

> **"**
> *I have to be careful not to let my passport expire as I'm not sure I have all the documents needed to reapply. My birth certificate from Papua New Guinea has been problematic.*
> Marco, 64
> – 11 years with a missionary organisation, 5 years with the ADF

Driver's licences

A driver's licence is really important when returning to Australia. I (Tanya) got my licence as soon as I could – learner's licence at 16, provisional licence at 17, full licence at 20. I (Kath) didn't get my licence until I was 18, which was seen as lazy. The truth is, I had other people running me around and I didn't need to get it fast.

Why do most Australians get driving licences so young? Because for many people, private transport is the only efficient, reliable way to get around. Most cities have public transport, but in some states public transport is not as good as in others. The more rural the area you live in, the less likely you are to have decent public transport available. Getting yourself around – by walking, riding a bike, or driving a car – is usually your best bet. When I (Kath) did decide to get my driver's licence, it was because I was starting university. My uni was an hour away by car, but nearly three hours by bus.

Each state and territory has its own rules, so it is important to go to the state/territory government website for exact information. As of 2023, you can get a learner's licence at 16 years in most parts of Australia, the exception being the ACT, where you can get it at 15 years and 9 months. You need to be supervised up to the age of 18 in Victoria, 16 years and 6 months in the NT, and 17 years elsewhere. After passing a test at the conclusion of your learning period, a three-year provisional period applies before you can receive a full licence. This provisional period applies up to a minimum age, even if you had a driving licence in another country before returning to Australia.

> **"**
> *I had a full driver's licence from the US yet had to go all the way back to the start of the three years of the provisional licence upon returning to Australia because I was under a certain age. I should be done at this point; instead I have another two years to go. No official was willing to help me, and many wanted me back on my learner's.*
> Tayo, 21
> – 6 years with the ADF

What is most important is that in order to get an Australian driver's licence, you must have an Australian residential address. One TCK I (Kath) know used their grandparents' address to get their licence. Most states and the territories want you to have 100 points of identification to prove who you are before granting your licence.

> **❝**
> *Getting my driver's licence was a little intimidating. I'm glad my parents helped me point out where to stand in line, or what I needed to bring to pay for what was required of me.*
> Opal, 28
> – 15 years with a missionary organisation

The identity requirement for driver's licences is strict because moving forward, your driver's licence will be an important form of identification (Australia does not have a national ID card). That said, you don't have to drive or get a licence in Australia. 6% of our cohort have never had an Australian driver's licence. Proof of Age cards (photo identification cards that look similar to driving licences) are issued by the states and territories in much the same way that driving licences are issued – without the driving test!

If you get a driver's licence outside Australia, you may still be able to use it to drive in Australia. You will need to check the rules for the state/territory you will be driving in.

> **❝**
> *My Australian driver's licence was transferred from my first country many years ago. It's hard to renew it from overseas.*
> Marco, 64
> – 11 years with a missionary organisation, 5 years with the ADF

> **❝**
> *You could drive for a long time on Alberta's graduated driver's licence (it's similar to the provisional licence in Australia) but I intentionally went for my full licence because it's easier to transfer if I ever change countries.*
> Lyndall, 30
> – 5 years for family reasons

Learning to drive in Australia

Each state and territory has a different process for licensing new drivers, including a different minimum age. As a learner driver, you must be under the supervision of someone with a full licence (not a provisional or expired licence). The age of the supervisor is not at issue, but the type of licence they hold. For example, if you are 21 when you begin learning, a person who is also 21 but holds a full licence can serve as your supervisor. You do not need a single 'sponsor' to supervise you; you can have a different supervisor every time you drive. For example, when my (Tanya's) youngest sister learned to drive, her supervisors were her paid driving instructor, our mother, our father, and me.

> **"**
> *I don't drive here because I don't really have parents that can take me on driving lessons. I know how to drive but it's a very big thing that you have to do, and it's very helpful to have a safety net.*
> Cardamon, 23
> – 11 years in aid and development

There are three different stages you need to go through to get your full driver's licence:
1. Learner's licence – L plates*
2. Provisional licence – Red Ps*
3. Provisional licence – Green Ps*

L Plates

Once you pass a written test, you receive a learner's licence. During this stage you must display square yellow signs with a big black L in the centre, called L plates*, on the front and back of any vehicle you are driving. This stage is therefore called being 'on your Ls*'. You have one year to complete the requirements, or you will need to renew your learner's licence. (This is important for Australian TCKs trying to acquire a licence through visits.)

Most states and territories require the completion of a 'log book' in which your supervisor attests to the number of hours you have spent practising your driving, and in which conditions. For example, learner drivers in NSW must log at least 120 hours of driving including 20 hours of night driving.

Red Ps

When you have completed your state or territory's requirements (including any log book requirements), you take a practical test to gain your provisional licence. It is not uncommon to fail your practical test – even more than once!

> **66**
> *I found it very hard to get my Australian driver's licence having previously learned to drive in Manila. I had great awareness and control, but no understanding/respect for road rules in Australia. I failed the driving test three times which was very discouraging.*
> John, 28
> – 3 years with a missionary organisation

> **66**
> *I failed the first test for getting my Ls once, but the driving test for the red Ps was fine.*
> Johnny, 36
> – 18 years for family reasons

Once you have a provisional licence, you may drive on your own, without supervision. During this stage you must display square white signs with a big red P in the centre, called P plates*, on the front and back of any vehicle you are driving. This stage is therefore called being 'on your Ps'. There are still limitations, though again these vary somewhat depending on your state/territory. For the first year of your Ps, you must display red P plates. You may have fewer demerit points available on your licence (we will talk about demerits soon), and you cannot drink anything prior to driving. You may not use a mobile phone device at all, including hands free, during this stage. There are also restrictions on who can be a passenger in your car at night.

Green Ps

For the final two years of your Ps, you must display green P plates – a white square with a green P in the centre. Some states will let you progress to your Green Ps earlier by taking a defensive driving course.

You may now use a mobile phone device hands free and have no restrictions on carrying passengers at night. The restriction against using any alcohol before driving still stands.

How to lose your licence in one easy step

One last word on driving in Australia: there are significant consequences to breaking road rules in Australia. While some countries are a bit loose in their interpretation and application of road rules, Australia is not one of them. There are a lot of speed cameras around the country (both mobile police stops with radar trackers and 24-hour cameras), and the faster you drive, the higher the penalty will be. Most speed cameras are signposted, but they aren't always easy to spot. The same goes for being caught driving with alcohol in your system: there are regular RBTs* (Random Breath Tests), and the more over the limit you are, the higher the penalty.

Generally speaking, a full licence starts with 12 points. A learner has five points per year; a provisional driver has five points per year, or 12 points per three years. If you lose all your points within a three-year period, your licence will be revoked and you have to reapply by taking the driving tests again.

Most driving infractions cost three demerit points and a significant fine ($300–$500). During peak travel periods (such as over long weekends and during school holidays) it is common for police to declare a 'double demerit*' period, where both the demerit points and monetary fines for all infractions are doubled.

If you speed through an intersection trying to catch an orange light and are caught more than 10 km/h over the limit while running a red light, that will cost you six demerit points. (Driving through an orange is okay, but be careful – you cannot be inside the intersection when the light turns red.) If you are on a learner or provisional licence, this is enough for your licence to be revoked. If it is a double demerit weekend, even a full licence will be revoked due to that one incident.

We share this not to scare you, but to give you a sense of how strictly Australia takes its road rules. The bottom line is that when driving in

Australia, know the rules and drive according to them and you'll be fine! I (Tanya) lost a total of four points in my six years as a young driver in Australia and only one point in six years as an older driver in Australia.

myGov

Developed in 2013, myGov is an online portal for accessing Australia's government services for individuals. It doesn't really 'do' anything, but is a tool to connect many federal government services in one place. This will be your first port of call for many services discussed in the rest of this section. 91% of our cohort have a myGov account, and another 4% used one in the past.

66
I think it is helpful to have one central portal for different government agencies you have to contact/access.
Johnny, 36
– 18 years for family reasons

From the age of 14 you can create your own myGov account. All you need is your own email address, then go to my.gov.au and follow the prompts to create your account. In theory, it is pretty easy. However not everyone finds it straightforward in practice – especially since we don't all fit the boxes neatly!

Once you have myGov set up, you can link any other account you create (Medicare, Centrelink, Tax Office, etc.) and access everything in one place. As with every online service, some things about the system are really convenient, whereas other things are less helpful, especially if you don't have the paperwork the system expects you to have! Getting it set up properly is worth the effort, however.

66
MyGov is the most annoying and convoluted website ever. I feel like all the government websites and systems could be a whole lot less confusing.
Amelie, 18
– 10 years with a missionary organisation

> **"**
> *MyGov is not exactly user-friendly, but I've had to use worse in the past.*
> Derek, 45
> – 10 years with a missionary organisation

If you find yourself stuck, don't be afraid to ask a friend to help you, or call their helpline. This goes not only for myGov, but for all the government services we will talk about in the rest of this section. Sometimes the system just isn't set up for people with international lives – it might ask for an answer you can't give, for example. In these cases, a person on the other end may need to press some buttons with admin access for it to let you move forward. I (Tanya) am speaking from experience here!

Tax File Number

In Australia, once you earn a wage (even part-time) you need to pay tax. One of the first things you need is a Tax File Number (TFN). The TFN identifies you for tax and superannuation purposes. It is yours for life. You keep the same TFN even if you change your name, change jobs, move interstate, or go overseas. It is comparable to the USA's Social Security Number, though with fewer uses. Whenever you get a job in Australia, you will be asked to provide your TFN. 91% of our cohort have a valid TFN, and another 5% used one in the past.

From the age of 15 you may get a job in Australia without your employer requiring a 'child employment permit'. Therefore, at 15 you may also apply for a TFN. This application is free and can be done online using your myGov ID once it is set up. You will need to have your Australian passport and another form of identification ready (such as your birth certificate or driver's licence).

Background checks

On occasion, you may need to get a background check and obtain a document proving you have not committed a crime and/or are considered legally safe to work with children or other vulnerable people.

There are two main types of checks you may apply for in Australia: a *national level* police check, and a *state level* background check for working with children/vulnerable people. The national check is what you need for visa purposes and other international level purposes, as well as some high-security jobs. The state level check is required for various jobs (including volunteer roles) in Australia. These checks are usually quite simple to apply for online if you have Australian identification documents. 74% of our cohort have applied for a national level check, and 83% have applied for a state level check.

The national level check is provided by the Australian Federal Police. When searching for this, be certain to visit the AFP's official website. There are a lot of other services (with Google ads that look like search results) that will promise to get you a police check, while charging you twice the price. More information about the national police check: afp.gov.au/what-we-do/national-police-checks

State level checks are different for every state and territory – they even have different names. I (Kath) am sure the name changes every time I renew mine! For example, in NSW and SA it is a Working With Children Check (WWCC); in the ACT it is a Working With Vulnerable People (WWVP) registration. If an employer requests one from you, they should be able to tell you the name of the document and where to get it. If in doubt, go to the website for government services in your state or territory. These checks are usually valid for a certain time period (usually a few years), after which time they need to be renewed or will expire. You should get a registration number and/or a physical card.

Chapter 9:

Your Responsibilities as an Australian

Citizenship comes with responsibilities. Some are legal requirements and some are social obligations. In some countries, citizenship comes with the responsibility to undertake military service, for example. We will not go over Australia's whole legal code (which applies to everyone who visits Australia, not just citizens!), but we will take this opportunity to discuss bills, taxes, and voting.

Paying bills

Paying bills is part of life everywhere in the world. What not everyone realises, however, is that bills are administered differently in different parts of the world. While some are pre-paid (paying for utilities/services before you use them) in Australia, the majority are post-paid – with a bill sent to you showing the exact amount used during a certain period, and how much you owe the company providing the utility/service. This means it's important to keep track of what the services you use cost, so that you don't accidentally use so much that you get a huge bill at the end of the period.

In Australia, most bills are paid electronically. Payment by cash or cheque is extremely rare. In most cases this means a bank transfer – a free service provided by most banks, including smaller banks and credit unions. The person or company you are paying will give you the BSB (Bank State Branch, an identification number for Australian banks) and the Account Number to send the money to, and your bank's online banking system will let you enter that information to send a free electronic funds transfer.

A similar system for paying companies is BPAY. If the company offers BPAY, you can pay them with an online transfer. Log into your bank's online banking system, select the BPAY option, and enter the BPAY Biller Code the company provided on their invoice to set up an online transfer.

Some companies prefer – or require – a direct debit. Setting this up means sending them your banking information, and they will take money from your account on a regular schedule. If you have a direct debit set up, it is vital to make sure you have enough money in the account to cover payments. Many banks will charge you a fee if a payment is charged that your account cannot cover.

> **"**
> *Usually you will either get a letter or an email that lets you know your bill information – how much it costs – and then you can either set up a direct debit so that it's automatically taken out of your account, or use BPAY, which is super helpful because you can just send it in your own time or whenever your bill is due. The problem with direct debits is if the money in your account fluctuates, or it's connected to an account you don't keep a lot of money in, you might not have enough on the day the money is taken out. Then they call you asking when you're going to pay your bill.*
> Cardamon, 23
> – 11 years in aid and development

Paying tax

As soon as you get a job in Australia you will need to pay tax. I (Kath) started paying tax at the age of 14 when I got my first job at Coles Supermarket as a checkout operator. Paying tax is something that often scares people, especially young adults who are new to earning income – or new to the country altogether. This section is here to calm your fears and equip you with knowledge and tools, so you know where to go to get the information you need. And don't forget: you can always ask someone for help!

> **"**
> *Paying tax was quite challenging. First, I had to call the tax office because my account wasn't linked to myGov so I couldn't access my statement. Then, filling it out was confusing as I still wasn't sure what to include and I was only working a casual job. Luckily my parents helped me a lot and checked that I did it all correctly. I advise keeping track of things that go into your tax*

over the year rather than getting stressed going over everything
from the year to find what is tax deductible.
Danielle, 19
– 11 years with a missionary organisation

If you've paid taxes before (in other countries) you may find the Australian tax system quite reasonable. There are always complications, but having done tax returns for three countries, I (Tanya) find the Australian system quite manageable.

"
Thankfully, Australia's tax is way easier than other places."
Cardamon, 23
– 11 years in aid and development

"
Paying taxes has gotten easier, especially since we can do it on
the ATO [Australian Tax Office] website now.
Johnny, 36
– 18 years for family reasons

The Australian financial year runs from July 1st to June 30th. Between July 1st and October 30th, you must lodge a tax return which reports your income for the preceding financial year and calculates the amount of tax you must pay. Four in 5 of our cohort have filed an Australian tax return.

You can lodge your taxes online on your own, or through a tax agent (an accountant who can help you prepare and lodge your tax return, whether you connect with them online or in person). If your income is derived from only a few sources and there are no major complications to your situation, the online lodgement tool provided by the Australian Tax Office (ATO) is a great free option.

"
Paying my tax in Australia was not too difficult because my
income was simple. There's lots of information sheets online.
Olivia, 23
– 10 years with a missionary organisation

There are also tax accounting firms who file taxes on your behalf for reasonable rates; I (Kath) pay about $100 per year to my tax firm. You can log into the ATO online portal at <u>ato.gov.au</u> – a service that can be linked to myGov – and follow step-by-step instructions, with links to more information explaining all the taxation terms used.

> **"**
> *Unless you have a regular job where your income tax is deducted automatically, it's well worthwhile finding a good tax accountant to help you complete your tax return each year. It is a very complex and confusing tax system here.*
> Tamar, 50
> – 18 years in the business sector

Tax rates

There is an income threshold below which Australians are not taxed. In 2023, this income threshold was $18,000. If your annual income is below this threshold, you will not be taxed, but you still need to submit a tax return demonstrating this. 13% of our cohort had filed tax returns but not had to pay taxes as they had not met the income threshold. Above the taxable threshold, the tax rate increases with your income, but is broken into stages – so you can't earn less if you get a pay increase that puts you into a new tax bracket!

If you have earned above the taxation threshold and have not paid taxes through the year (or did not pay enough) you will have a tax bill to pay. If you overpaid through the year, you may receive a tax return – a reimbursement for overpaying your taxes. Most Australian employers automatically deduct taxes from your paycheck so that you do not end up with a large bill when you lodge your taxes. I (Kath) have one of my employers pay double tax on my behalf, which means I often get a little bit back at the end of the year. If you are self-employed or work overseas, however, you must pay more attention. You may need to set aside money as you go to cover your tax obligations at the end of the year.

As an Australian citizen, you need to report your income for the purpose of taxes every year, no matter where in the world you live or where you make your money. You will be taxed on any income earned inside Australia even if you are not an Australian resident (you must declare any change in residency). Foreign-earned income must also be declared, regardless of your residency, as it is potentially liable to Australian taxes (after taking into account any taxes you have already paid in another country). For more information about tax obligations for Australians living overseas, see ato.gov.au/Individuals/coming-to-australia-or-going-overseas

Paying tax is important. Those who are fortunate to have more than enough are able to support those who are less fortunate, creating a society that is more well-funded on the whole. Australian taxes pay for services such as education, health, defence, and infrastructure (roads, bridges, and utility networks).

Voting

Australians over the age of 18 are required to enrol to vote, with very few exceptions. Once you are on the electoral roll, you are required to vote in all federal and state elections; failure to vote will result in a fine. You must also keep your enrolment up to date, with your current residential/mailing address. At the time of our survey, 87% of our cohort were registered to vote in Australia, and another 7% had previously been on the electoral roll.

You can enrol to vote any time after you turn 16, but you can only vote in an election after turning 18. If you are over 18 and have never enrolled, you can enrol now and you will not be penalised. If you are an Australian citizen over 18 who has been living overseas since before you turned 18, you have one parent on the Australian electoral roll, and you intend to return to live in Australia within six years after your 18th birthday, you can enrol now.

Enrol to vote or update your enrolment online at aec.gov.au

Australia's voting system

Many countries have different systems of government, including different parliaments and different systems for elections/voting. Australia uses 'preferential voting'. This is different to the 'first past the post' system used by many countries, where the candidate with the most votes wins, and it is important to understand the difference – especially if you missed learning about this in an Australian school!

> **"**
> *I have voted, once federally and once in my state. I don't know a lot about the electoral system as I never studied politics during school, but I know which policies are important to me and I am able to keep track of what the parties are doing about each of them, which helps my decisions.*
> Danielle, 19
> – 11 years with a missionary organisation

The basic premise of preferential voting is that your vote is always counted, even if your preferred candidate does not win. You mark your top candidate with a [1] and then choose your next favourite with a [2]. Then you keep going, numbering the candidates according to your preferences. This way, even if the vote comes down to your second least favourite candidate against your least favourite candidate, you still get a say. No matter who the final contest is between, your voice is heard.

When votes are counted, there are often multiple rounds of counting. In the first round, all votes are assigned to their first preference – the candidates marked with a [1]. If no candidate has more than 50% of the vote, the candidate with the fewest [1] votes is taken out of the running, and these votes are reassigned to the second preferences marked – the candidates marked [2]. Again, if there is no candidate with over 50% of the vote, the candidate with the fewest votes is taken out of the running and their votes reassigned to the next preference. This 'flow of preferences' often determines the outcome of an election. This is a simplified explanation – to learn more, visit aec.gov.au/learn/preferential-voting.htm

This system of voting encourages the election of minor parties and independents. While Australia has two major parties (one being a coalition of two parties with similar policies), there are also several minor parties with seats in the government, and a number of independents.

Most elections in Australia are said to be between 'Labor' and 'The Coalition'. The Australian Labor Party (the ALP, and yes, that's how it's spelled) is a centre-left party. The Liberal Party (confusingly a conservative party) is aligned with the National Party. These two parties work together in a coalition, usually called The Coalition, with the Liberals generally representing urban electorates, and the Nationals generally representing rural electorates. Even though the ALP typically holds more seats than either the Liberal or National parties, together The Coalition can hold enough seats to gain governance.

The key minor party as of 2023 is the Australian Greens (a left-wing party); also notable is One Nation (a far-right party known for exclusionist policies and racist commentary). Smaller parties are often networks of independents associated with a specific leader (such as One Nation's Pauline Hanson), or single-issue parties angling for a senate seat (such as Legalise Cannabis Australia).

66
We have a compulsory voting system, which is good for getting everybody to participate in the democratic process, but since you have to give a preference for all the parties on the ballot paper, even parties you do not approve of at all, your vote can end up as a vote for a party that you are against, which I think is a flaw in the system.
Johnny, 36
– 18 years for family reasons

Election day

There are some pre-poll/postal vote options for elections in Australia (more on that a little later), but most people vote in person on the day. Elections in Australia are held on Saturdays. When you go to the polling place, you will be asked your name and to confirm your address, then sent to a private booth to fill in your ballot. If you vote outside your state, you must find a polling place that is assigned for out-of-state voters, so that they will have the correct forms available. (While there have been trials of electronic voting in some areas, as of 2023, federal elections use paper forms.) There will be volunteers for various candidates standing outside with information should you want to know more. There are rules about how close they can stand and what they can say.

"
My political views have changed a lot since I first moved here. Back then, I thought, 'I don't want to vote, I don't like anybody.' There are some good policies, but ultimately half the policies aren't great. Now I vote for the policies that are important to me and can only hope the government will keep their promises.
Cardamon, 23
– 11 years in aid and development

"
I really recommend you research the politicians before voting. The voting process is quite straightforward because there are people at the voting booths who explain it to you. But to actually vote you need previous knowledge about what the politicians stand for before going in.
Opal, 28
– 15 years with a missionary organisation

"
Read widely in the news, realise that no party is perfect, and vote according to which has most alignment with your values.
Marco, 64
– 11 years with a missionary organisation, 5 years with the ADF

Democracy sausages

One fun thing to know about Australian elections is that many primary schools are assigned to be polling places. Since many people are required to go there and stand in line to vote, these primary schools take the opportunity to run fundraisers – making money through cake stalls and sausage sizzles*. There are often other food options, drinks, games for kids, and more.

A sausage sizzle, if you aren't aware, is an Australian 'delicacy' – a barbecued sausage on a piece of white bread with a splash of tomato sauce, and optionally some grilled onions. The polling place sausage sizzle has become so much a part of the Australian electoral landscape that they have been nicknamed 'democracy sausages', and it is not uncommon to be asked if you got your democracy sausage over the weekend!

"
Voting is compulsory here, and election days are a big deal, especially state and federal elections. The whole community gets into the spirit of things – hence the sausage sizzles*, cake sales, etc.
Tamar, 50
– 18 years in the business sector

"
A 'democracy sausage' is an institution in which, after voting in a government election, you grab a sausage at the sausage sizzle stall outside. Often the stalls are run by local charities or not-for-profits accepting gold coin donations*. It is not, however, known everywhere. North Queensland is sadly yet to take up this tradition!
Claire, 27
– 9 years with a missionary organisation

Voting when you are away

If you are outside Australia during an election (including the two weeks prior to the election, when pre-poll voting is available) you are not required to vote. You are able to vote by means of a postal vote, or by visiting a designated embassy/consulate acting as a federal polling place. Most international polling places are open for two weeks prior to a federal election. I (Tanya) have voted in an Australian federal election at the Australian Embassy in Beijing. When I (Kath) voted in a federal election at the Australian Embassy in Cambodia they had a sausage sizzle. It was so good to get my democracy sausage even overseas!

Sometimes the Australian government gets its wires crossed! I (Tanya) was once mailed a fine notice for not voting – when I was overseas! The fine was dismissed with proof that I was out of the country during the election.

"
My parents got a letter from the government when we first moved asking why they didn't vote – due to mandatory voting they were going to get a fine. They explained that we were thousands of kilometres away.
Lyndall, 30
– 5 years for family reasons

Governance

Understanding at least the basics of how Australian governance works is important for all Australian citizens, no matter where you live. I (Kath) often get confused about exactly how the Australian Government works – and I have lived here most of my life! That might be because when we were taught about Australian politics in school, I would be drawing or getting distracted very easily. I (Tanya) have clear memories of government classes in Grade 6, mainly because I got to be Speaker of our 'mock parliament' – a common way politics is taught to Australian students. But I missed later discussion of Australian politics because I was living outside Australia during those years.

> **"**
> *I learned very little about Australia's history and the political system. Canada has a relatively similar political system to Australia thanks to both countries being part of the Commonwealth, but I only know the broadest overview; I don't know any sort of specifics about how the electoral and judicial systems work in Australia. This makes it hard to be informed about any sort of political stuff.*
> Lyndall, 30
> – 5 years for family reasons

Australia is a representative democracy. This means we vote for leaders to represent our interest in the government, and those representatives choose their own leader. So Australians do not directly choose the leader of their government; instead, the leader of the party in power is the Prime Minister of the country. The Australian Prime Minister can therefore change within the government's term of office. At one stage while living in Cambodia, I (Kath) could not even remember who our Prime Minister was due to mid-term changes!

There are three different levels of government in Australia: federal, state, and local. We vote for representatives in each of these levels. We'll give you a basic run down here, and you can learn more at the Parliamentary Education Office website: peo.gov.au

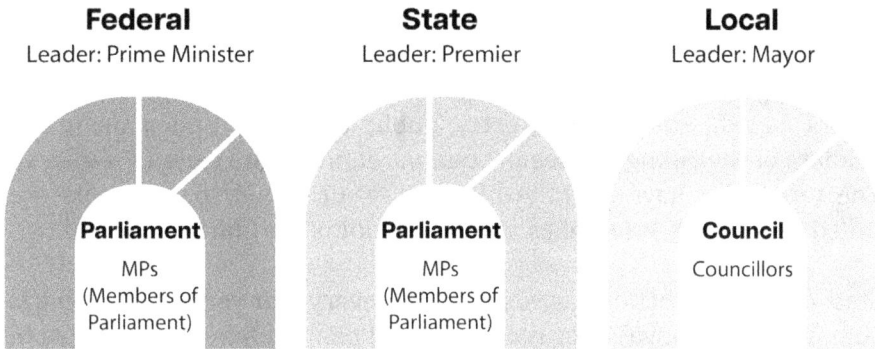

Federal Leader: Prime Minister	**State** Leader: Premier	**Local** Leader: Mayor
Parliament MPs (Members of Parliament)	**Parliament** MPs (Members of Parliament)	**Council** Councillors

In state parliaments, the leader of the ruling party is called the Premier.
The territories are slightly different. Their parliaments are called Legislative
Assemblies and their leaders are Chief Ministers**

Federal government

The Federal Government makes decisions for the whole of Australia, and looks after social security, industrial relations, foreign affairs, trade, immigration, and national defence. The ruling party is the government, their leader is the Prime Minister*, and the Prime Minister's key leaders are the Cabinet Ministers.

The largest minority party is called the opposition, their leader is the Leader of the Opposition, and their key leaders are the Shadow Cabinet Ministers.

There are two bodies to make decisions: the House of Representatives and the Senate. Electorates that elect Members of Parliament to seats in the House of Representatives are determined by population, with each MP representing an approximately equal number of constituents.

The 76 Australian Senate seats are designed to give each state an equal say, regardless of population. 12 senators are assigned to each state of Australia, and two each for the NT and ACT.

Australia holds a federal election every three years, though the exact date is determined by the government (within a set date range), and voting is compulsory. Senators have six-year terms, so only half the senate seats are up for election at any one time.

State government

The state governments operate similarly, and look after justice, consumer affairs, health, education, forestry, public transport, and main roads. Leaders of the ruling parties in state parliaments are called Premiers*. The territories have slightly different set-ups; their parliaments are called Legislative Assemblies and their leaders are Chief Ministers*.

State/territory elections are usually held every four years, and voting is compulsory. I (Tanya) once received – and paid – a fine for not voting in an ACT election because while I was away during the election itself, pre-poll voting opened a few days before I left!

Local government

Finally, there is the local government, with responsibility for local road maintenance, rubbish collection, building regulations, land subdivisions, public health, and recreation facilities such as swimming pools.

Local governing bodies are usually called local councils, and these are responsible for Local Government Areas (LGAs). Their representatives are councillors, and their leader is the mayor. Voting in local elections may be compulsory or optional, depending on where you live. These are the governing bodies where decisions most close to home happen. If you want something done or fixed in your community, the first stop is usually your local council.

66

Spending so much time in other countries, you see they aren't as great as they may appear when you just visit for a short period of time. Especially now that I'm studying politics, I'm really starting to appreciate the system we have here in Australia. That's really helping me in grappling with my Australian-ness.
Nathan, 28
– 5 years with a missionary organisation

Chapter 10:

Resources Available to You as an Australian Citizen 'At Home'

As an Australian citizen, you have the right to access a range of services when you are in Australia. Most of these services are not available when you live outside Australia, but once you are back in the country, the amount of time you lived abroad does not disqualify you (in most cases – occasionally there is a waiting period).

> **❝**
> *I always appreciated Australia's social services, even when they were frustrating or inefficient because I grew up in a place without any of those for the citizens.*
> Elliot, 35
> – 11 years with a missionary organisation

> **❝**
> *I think Australia's social services are invaluable.*
> Shellie, 54
> – 1 year with the ADF

Navigating the systems for accessing these services can be daunting, however. In this section, we have gathered an overview of these services, with some advice about accessing them – along with stories about experiences other Australian TCKs have had while trying to access services. We want you to be confident about accessing the services you are entitled to as an Australian citizen, even if it takes a bit of extra effort, given your TCK background.

> **❝**
> *When applying for benefits in Australia, I am immediately questioned about my legal status because I do not have an Australian accent. Because I have an American accent, I have to prove my rights as an Australian, and fight for benefits that I have a right to.*
> Darren, 38
> – 17 years in the education sector

"
I have taught my kids (also TCKs) to document everything – especially interactions with Centrelink – and advocate for themselves (contact various agencies multiple times as needed) to get the services/advice they need.
Annie, 52
– 8 years with the education sector

Emergency services

As these types of services are different in every country, we felt it was important to start with emergencies! Australia has great emergency services. The main services are the police, ambulance, and firefighting services. In general, Australia's emergency services personnel are safe people to approach when you need help of any kind. If they do not have the answer (or aren't the right person to ask), they can point you in the right direction. If you need help, going into a police or fire station is safe. We say this knowing it is not the case in all countries, including the countries you may be coming from.

Triple zero (000) is the general emergency number in Australia. 112 is the number to call if you do not have service on your mobile; this will go directly to the emergency number. Call triple zero (000) for assistance from ambulance, police, or fire services if you are in a situation that is serious and urgent. This includes serious injuries and urgent medical needs, imminent threat to life or property, and witnessing a serious accident or crime. If a situation is not urgent, you can look up the phone number of local services – the police, firefighting, and ambulance services in each local area have their own local numbers for non-emergency situations. Learn more about emergency calls at acma.gov.au/emergency-calls

To look up other emergency services in your state/territory, see triplezero.gov.au/triple-zero/regional-services

Police

While the police service in Australia is not perfect, it is safe to approach the police and ask for help. They will not ask for (nor expect) bribes of any kind. You can ask for help from the police in non-emergency situations and for general assistance with non-criminal matters. They will be able to point you in the right direction.

The general number for police assistance is 131 444. If you are experiencing an emergency, such as witnessing a crime or serious accident, you can also contact the police through 000.

Ambulance

When you need an ambulance for a medical emergency, call 000. Ambulances are also used for non-emergency situations, such as for patient transport, but this is organised through your regular medical practitioner.

There is a fee for ambulance transfers in some states. In most states, holding a concession card (if you receive welfare payments through Centrelink, you will be given the option to apply for a concession card as well) entitles you to free ambulance rides. In some states, all residents receive free ambulance transfers. In other states, private health insurance will cover the cost of ambulance transfer, or you can sign up for ambulance membership. Be sure to check the situation where you live and travel.

State Emergency Service

Another emergency service to be aware of is the State Emergency Service (SES), which is made up of volunteers who provide a range of practical support in emergency situations, such as floods and storms. The SES can be reached at 132 500.

Rural Fire Service

Bushfires are emergencies that occur frequently in Australia. The Rural Fire Service (RFS) is another volunteer organisation and works to protect communities from grass fires and bushfires that might otherwise threaten homes (and lives). Generally speaking, Fire and Rescue services are responsible for urban areas, and the RFS is responsible for rural areas – which means that while the Fire and Rescue service fights most house/building fires, the RFS takes care of most of the country's bushfire prevention.

Learning about bushfires – what they are, how to prevent them, and what to do if you are near one – is important when living in Australia. The Australian Climate Service (ACS) website has helpful information, including how to learn more about the services in each state/territory. Some states have websites/apps that alert you to nearby bushfires. acs.gov.au/pages/bushfires

Another useful source of information is the Australian Institute for Disaster Resilience (AIDR) website:
knowledge.aidr.org.au/resources/bushfire/

Banking

A bank account is important for paying bills and receiving funds. Australia's international banking laws can complicate sending/receiving money internationally, so having a local bank account makes life easier. Opening a bank account in Australia is very easy and inexpensive (usually a minimum deposit of $25–$100), which is a relief compared to other places where I (Tanya) have tried to open bank accounts!

There are four major banks in Australia, commonly called 'The Big Four', which have branches and ATMs all over the country. They are:

♦ The Australia and New Zealand Banking Group (ANZ Bank)
♦ Commonwealth Bank of Australia (CommBank or CBA)
♦ National Australia Bank (NAB)
♦ Westpac

There are also many other banks and credit unions/building societies (customer-owned banks) you may want to check out; these often have lower fees and better interest rates. Banks may levy fees for things such as: monthly account use, using an ATM, too many transactions, insufficient funds for an attempted transaction, overdraft fees, and more. Examples of other banks include AMP, Bankwest, Bank of Queensland, Bendigo Bank, HSBC, ING, Macquarie Bank, and Suncorp. Some credit unions are only open to people in a certain group (such as the Teachers Mutual Bank and Australian Military Bank); others are open to all, such as Australian Unity, Bank Australia, G&C Mutual Bank, Great Southern Bank, Hume Bank, and Qudos.

The Big Four banks (and many others) allow non-residents to open an Australian bank account online before arriving in Australia. In five short steps, here's the easiest way to open an Australian bank account online:

1. Go to the website of the bank you have chosen. From there you will be able to fill in the details they need. If you prefer to do it over the phone, most banks will have contact numbers. Make sure to call within Australian business hours!

2. This will usually include providing 100 points of identification, and your tax registration number (TFN if you are Australian).

3. If you are not yet in Australia, make sure you know your exact arrival date in Australia. In some cases you will need to provide this date to the bank when you apply for an account. Some banks will not require this if you are applying from overseas.

4. Have an Australian mailing address ready before you apply. In most cases, all they require is a mailing address – not a Post Office (PO) box* – where you can receive mail. You should not need to prove residency. Some banks will allow you to sign up for a bank account online shortly before you arrive without yet having an Australian mailing address.

5. Scan and upload all requested documents, including your passport (and visa, in the case of non-citizens).

Once you are in Australia (and approved online), head to your nearest branch to verify your documents and complete your application. You will receive a physical bank card as well as access to an online banking system, and probably an app for accessing online banking from your smartphone.

(Transfers through online banking is the most common way for friends to send each other money, so this is an important step.)

Medicare

Something I (Kath) have come to realise as I speak to friends overseas is how good our public healthcare is here in Australia. It is affordable and safe, and the quality is great. All Australians can visit doctors or public hospitals and receive subsidised (or even completely free) medical care. The system is not perfect, but there is a medical safety net that covers us all. Making sure you have a valid Medicare card, and keeping it with you, is very important when living in Australia. At the time of our survey, 92% of our cohort had a valid Medicare card, and another 7% had previously held a Medicare card; almost all had made use of the system.

> **"**
> *Medicare is an amazing system. It was a little bit difficult to set up but nonetheless it is definitely worth it, especially for those who can't afford private healthcare. It is really easy. All you have to do is carry around your Medicare card.*
> Milly, 21
> – 10 years for family reasons

> **"**
> *All aspects of healthcare can be challenging to access if English is not your first language, but there are multilingual language supports in place for those who require them.*
> Tamar, 50
> – 18 years in the business sector

Medicare is technically a health insurance scheme that the government funds through taxpayer contributions (this is a nationwide fund, not tied to your individual income). It gives Australians access to a wide range of health and hospital services, either free or at a subsidised cost. This includes services provided by your doctor, plus specialists and treatment with registered providers (such as audiology, chiropractic, dieticians, midwifery, obstetrics, occupational therapy, orthoptics, osteopathy, podiatry, and social work). It also includes free treatments at public hospitals and subsidised prescription medication. Another thing covered by Medicare is pathology (like blood tests) and scans (such as ultrasounds, CT scans, X-rays, and MRIs).

In some cases these services will be 'bulk-billed', meaning the bill goes straight to Medicare without you paying anything upfront. 83% of our cohort have received bulk-billed services. In other cases, you will be asked to pay the bill yourself, and then receive a portion back from Medicare. 47% of our cohort have managed payment this way.

There is a parallel private hospital system in Australia, with clinics and practitioners working outside the Medicare system. By paying these practitioners directly (or through private health insurance) you can plan your treatment to take place more quickly, with specific doctors, or in other ways most convenient to you. This is often very expensive, however.

In recent years, it has become harder to see a doctor without needing to pay a 'gap' fee (a charge higher than the Medicare rebate) to cover the costs of their practice, as the Medicare rebate has been capped for a long time and has not kept up with inflation. Depending on where you live, it may be difficult to find providers offering fully subsidised medical care, but you will still receive a subsidy through Medicare.

> **"**
> Medicare covers hospital treatments and certain doctor appointments for my family. I would say overall it is helpful as it can reduce some extreme medical costs. In the end though we pay taxes to the government who pay when you use Medicare.
> Danielle, 19
> – 11 years with a missionary organisation

> **"**
> *Medicare is a great service that helps subsidise costs.*
> Marco, 64
> – 11 years with a missionary organisation, 5 years with the ADF

Handling payments

Most medical services require you to pay upfront, while others will send you a bill (this is more common for hospital services and pathology/blood tests). When you pay upfront, your rebate (partial refund) from

Medicare is usually sent to you automatically and will be in your bank account within a day – sometimes immediately (register your bank details with your online Medicare account to receive these rebates). Otherwise, you will need to submit a claim to Medicare to receive the rebate.

Medicare claims can be done online, with a scan/photo of the receipt. You will also need to enter the Medicare claim number and the Medicare registration number of the healthcare provider. If you aren't sure where to find these numbers, ask the person who gives you the receipt to circle them for you. You cannot make a claim from an invoice/bill (where the medical provider asks you for payment) but only from a receipt (showing that you have made payment). If you pay a bill sent to you and are not provided with a receipt very quickly (usually within a few days), you can follow this up and ask for it.

Some tests and medications are *not* covered by Medicare. If a test is full fee, you will usually be told before it happens. If you are unsure, ask! I (Tanya) did a full battery of blood tests while experiencing long Covid symptoms. One of the 12 or so tests my doctor wanted was not covered under Medicare, and if I wanted to get it, I would need to pay for it myself. I was told before the test was done, so I could choose whether I wanted to pay or skip that test.

It is always okay to check what the cost of a test or procedure is before having it – at the time of the doctor's referral, and/or at the time you get the test – and what (if any) part Medicare covers. When I (Tanya) needed X-rays for a potentially broken ankle (it wasn't broken – I 'only' tore three ligaments!), I asked my doctor if it would be bulk-billed by the imaging clinic; my doctor wrote a note asking the clinic to bulk-bill me, and they did.

Subsidised medication

If you have a Medicare card, you also qualify for subsidised medication under the Pharmaceutical Benefits Scheme (PBS). This is a list of medications that the Australian government subsidises for its citizens, and is updated every month.

Australia also has a Reciprocal Health Care Agreement (RHCA) with several countries, meaning citizens of these countries are able to access PBS subsidies. As of 2023, the following countries have RHCAs with Australia: Belgium, Finland, Ireland, Italy, Malta, Netherlands, New Zealand, Norway, Slovenia, Sweden, and the United Kingdom.

> **"**
> *Medicare is a medical safety for all people for most significant medical things. Don't forget the PBS safety net as well! I think it is easy as most claims are automatic. Greatest weaknesses for me are so-called 'elective surgery,' increasing gap payments as Medicare hasn't increased recommended fees for most services, and waiting lists. I think it is very much worth it and it evens out some income inequalities.*
> Hurley, 64
> – 3 years with the ADF

Getting your own Medicare card

All Australian citizens are eligible for a Medicare card. Children under the age of 15 are listed on the card of their parent/guardian.

Assuming your parent is an Australian citizen, they probably have a Medicare card that lists you. If you are still on your parent's Medicare card, you will need your own one after the age of 15. If you are over 15, listed on only one Medicare card which has other people on it, and live in Australia, you can apply for your own card over the internet using myGov.

If you/they do not have a Medicare card, or the card has expired (not uncommon if you have lived overseas for a prolonged period), the process is a little more complicated. You will probably need to take your identity document to a Medicare office in person and fill in forms to organise your Medicare card. I (Tanya) had to do this when my own card expired, and while it required me to fill out forms and bring a lot of identity documents to the Medicare office, the process was completed fairly quickly.

Mental health support

We are adding information on mental health support for three main reasons.

1. **Proactive knowledge**

   It's really good to learn how to access mental health support *before* you need it. Once you're struggling, it's really hard to be proactive about learning what to do – all your energy goes into getting through the day!

2. **Helping others**

   You never know when a friend might confide that they are struggling. Knowing where to go, and how to ask for help, is important knowledge everyone should have.

3. **TCK pitfalls**

   Many TCKs need time and space in adulthood to process their childhood experiences. If they don't get this time and space, depression and anxiety are common responses.

   "
   I've met several TCKs (including myself) who struggled with mental health upon their return to Australia.
   Zara, 19
   – 5 years with a missionary organisation

   "
   I loved my childhood – it was an amazing experience to travel and live in different places – but it has lasting negative effects on my mental health.
   Mei Mei, 22
   – 10 years with a missionary organisation

   "
   I think there is a correlation and possible causation between some of my mental illness and my experience repatriating as a child. I had severe separation anxiety as a child, which still manifests in my 20s. I have social anxiety and struggle to maintain friendships for more than about three years (the standard DFAT travel time). I have generalised anxiety and depression which can be somewhat traced back to bullying at my Australian school.
   Rosie, 25
   – 6 years with DFAT

"
Repatriation as a child was horrid. I suffered from severe depression and cultural shock. No support was offered to me.
Heather, 47
– 13 years with a missionary organisation

Mental Health Care Plans

In Australia, mental health services provided by doctors, psychiatrists, psychologists, occupational therapists, and social workers may be subsidised through Medicare. Your GP* (General Practitioner – doctor) is the best first step for receiving subsidised mental health care. They will talk with you about your mental health concerns, give you a questionnaire to complete, and you will come up with a Mental Health Care Plan (MHCP) together – which will include goals for what you want to achieve through therapeutic support. Once approved, your plan will allow you to get six subsidised sessions with a psychologist; a check-in after that can approve an additional four sessions.

"
I think Australia is getting much better at recognising the importance of providing subsidised mental health support services. The best place to start is to talk to your GP about getting a mental health plan, as well as advice on which services to reach out to.
Tamar, 50
– 18 years in the business sector

"
I've seen a couple of GPs and psychologists in Australia about my mental health. I mostly saw the psychologist about disruptive PTSD flashbacks relating to a traffic accident my whole family witnessed when I was a teenager in which three men died pretty brutally. The psychologist was helpful, and I learnt lots of coping strategies for dealing with flashbacks. It was clear that she didn't understand my TCK perspective, however. If I was going to have a longer-term relationship with a psychologist, I would need someone who could understand that Cambodia is my heart country – a place where I feel safe and at home.
Katie, 24
– 14 years with a missionary organisation

"

A lot was happening in our lives, and I had a few days where I just wasn't coping. I talked to my doctor and asked if maybe it was a good time to see a psychologist. She said, 'I think any time is a good time to see a psychologist.' That was great. I had six telehealth sessions with a psychologist. She said, 'You've told me about all these different experiences of your life, and many of those things produce a high level of stress – change, transition, things like that.' It was so helpful.

Lucy, 38

– 9 years with a missionary organisation

Counselling

There is also a wide range of counselling services available in Australia, though these are not included in Medicare's subsidised services. No specific training or registration is required to use the title 'Counsellor' in Australia, but there are many courses and registrations available, such as a diploma or bachelor's in Counselling, and accreditation with the Australian Counselling Association (ACA). No referral is needed to see a counsellor; you can make an appointment at any time.

Social workers

An additional avenue of support many people do not consider is social work. Social workers are allied health professionals who provide counselling, information, and referrals to other services. Social workers help people to face life's challenges, improve their wellbeing, and work to ensure they are treated fairly.

There can be a stigma about seeing a social worker, but they are an amazing support for anyone who needs help connecting with the medical or mental health services they need, or to learn how to manage daily life in Australia. This is a perfect fit for many repatriating TCKs! I (Kath) am a certified social worker in Australia, and have worked in the areas of homelessness, alcohol and drug dependency, family violence, and counselling.

Many social workers can provide Medicare-assisted support. You can look for a suitable social worker near you through the Australian Association of Social Workers: aasw.asn.au/find-a-social-worker

66
Getting a good social worker honestly makes a big difference, especially if you're dealing with depression and anxiety. You literally know a bill was due two weeks ago but you cannot move to do it: there is a full wall between you and doing that task. When I accessed services to help with my mental health, they were really helpful in helping me find social workers. I had a social worker for a while where I would go in for an hour and he would just sit down with me and we would do my Centrelink. I would just sit there and tell him passwords and other information so that he could access it all and do it for me because I couldn't function.
Cardamon, 23
– 11 years in aid and development

More support services

Through the rest of this section, we're going to highlight a few Australian services we think are particularly helpful.

Head to Health
Head to Health is a service provided by the Australian Government Department of Health. It helps you find digital mental health services across the country. These digital services include research-based apps and online programs, online forums, phone/chat/email services, and trusted websites. More at headtohealth.gov.au

Headspace
Headspace, the National Youth Mental Health Foundation, is a great source of mental health support for young people in Australia. Headspace has been offering services to young people aged 12–25 in Australia since 2006. Their website has lots of information and online services, and they have in-person centres all around the country. Headspace also provides training and support to parents, educators, and others who work with young people in Australia. Visit their website at headspace.org.au

Beyond Blue
Australian charity Beyond Blue provides mental health support for all Australians, including those supporting loved ones who are struggling. There is information on various areas of interest, and a free short-session counselling service, with both a phone line and an online chat portal. Their website is beyondblue.org.au

Lifeline
Lifeline is an Australian charity providing phone and text counselling for those experiencing a mental health crisis. Their website is lifeline.org.au

moodgym
Another helpful resource is moodgym, an online interactive 'self-help' therapy tool developed by the Australian National University through 15 years of research. (By coincidence, Tanya was a participant in a study testing the moodgym program 20 years ago.) It teaches Cognitive Behaviour Therapy (CBT) skills; completion of two or more modules is associated with a lowering of depression and anxiety. Learn more at moodgym.com.au

TCK Training
Finally, if you would like to find something specific to TCKs (though not Australia-specific), check out TCK Training's resources for Adult TCKs. This includes free printable worksheets, lists of mental health services trained in TCK/expat life, and other resources: tcktraining.com/for-atcks

> **"**
> *Repatriation was incredibly challenging. I sought support from a psychologist early on who was not helpful as they didn't have the ability to relate to what I spoke about. Later I found another psychologist who was more empathetic. I found it hard though to talk about my 'problems' because people viewed my life as privileged.*
> Holly, 30
> – 8 years in the education sector

Private health insurance

Medicare provides a great safety net, especially for basic medical care and emergency procedures. Once you turn 30, a Medicare levy is added as part of your taxes (2% of income over the taxable threshold), but this is waived should you have your own private health cover.

> **"**
> *I don't have private health insurance, just because I don't see that there is a point just because Medicare is so good.*
> Milly, 21
> – 10 years for family reasons

> **"**
> *I have private health insurance, but it is mainly for my children and hospital cover. I don't think it is absolutely vital, but it is an added layer of peace of mind.*
> Tamar, 50
> – 18 years in the business sector

> **"**
> *We have private health insurance, as we have kids. It depends on the person as to whether I would recommend it. I do believe we have a great medical system here in Australia, for which I am very thankful, and Medicare is really good.*
> Sally, 52
> – 7 years with a missionary organisation

Basic private health insurance provides additional cover, especially for things like ambulance service, physiotherapy, remedial massage, dentistry, and optometry (glasses). More complete private healthcare packages will include greater coverage for hospital extras, including choosing particular doctors and specialists, being treated in private hospitals, and more. Some private health cover provides benefits for psychology services and other mental health support. I (Tanya) have a basic private health insurance policy that costs less than $40 a month. Dental work alone has more than covered that cost most years. I've also used it for physiotherapy, massage therapy, and to buy glasses.

> **❝**
> *Depending on income and health status, it may not be worth having private health cover – although access to medical treatment may be delayed without it.*
> Rho, 60+
> – 2 years in aid and development

> **❝**
> *Private healthcare gives me better optical and dental. And physiotherapist cover. Private hospital cover eliminates most waiting lists and reduces hospitalisation and ambulance costs greatly.*
> Hurley, 64
> – 3 years with the ADF

Many clinics that are usually subsidised by private health coverage have HICAPS machines (Health Industry Claims and Payment Service). These look like a normal EFTPOS* machine, but they read private health fund cards instead. We both regularly use this system to pay for our dental and physiotherapy appointments. If you believe your private health cover provides a discount, the person at reception can swipe your card through the HICAPS machine to get approval and payment directly from the private health fund on the spot. Similar to Medicare-subsidised treatments, this means you only have to pay the gap (any fee higher than your coverage) and do not need to file a claim with your health insurer.

One thing to keep in mind is that you cannot claim the same treatment on both Medicare and your private health insurance – it is one or the other. If a treatment you need qualifies to be subsidised by both, you must choose one. Compare the costs/limitations of each ahead of time so you can let your medical practitioner know whether you are going through the public or private system for your treatment.

National Disability Insurance Scheme (NDIS)

Over four million Australians have a disability. The NDIS provides funding directly to Australian individuals aged 7–65 living in Australia "who have a permanent and significant disability" to manage their support needs. Each person on the NDIS scheme has a written individual plan which is unique to their specific needs. Once the plan is approved, support offered by registered providers can be purchased to meet the goals laid out in the plan. There are also options for self-managed plans with more flexibility. Learn more about the NDIS at ndis.gov.au

Centrelink

Centrelink is the government body that provides social welfare payments and is another system connected to myGov. More than three-quarters of our cohort had received benefits from Centrelink, half of those from more than one service. Most Australians are of two minds when we talk about Centrelink: it is great to receive financial support, but getting that help requires jumping through innumerable hoops!

"
It can be so frustrating dealing with Centrelink.
Cardamon, 23
– 11 years in aid and development

"
I often do not know if I know as much as I should about what we should be applying for. Centrelink seems to be understaffed when I go to inquire and fairly dismissive.
Etta, 42
– 8 years with a missionary organisation

Common support payments

Youth Allowance is a payment for those under the age of 25 who are studying, in an apprenticeship, or looking for work. If you are over 25, different payments are available, such as Austudy for full-time students/ apprentices and JobSeeker when looking for work (if you're over 22). There are also payments to support parents with children under the age of six, people with disabilities or caring for those with disabilities (including a mobility payment if you cannot take public transport due to a disability), crisis payments for domestic abuse situations, and payments connected to the death of a loved one.

If you are a full-time student in a registered tertiary course of study – such as at university or technical college like TAFE* (Technical and Further Education) – you will generally be eligible for Youth Allowance or Austudy. This will depend on additional factors, such as how much you/your parents earn.

> **66**
>
> *I had support from Centrelink as a full-time undergraduate student.*
>
> Derek, 45
> – 10 years with a missionary organisation

I (Tanya) did not qualify for Youth Allowance during my undergrad due to my parents' income. When I got my master's degree, I had a three-month exclusion period before my Austudy payments began because I had money saved up in my bank account to pay for my accommodation. (Cash counts against you, including gifts, whereas concrete assets like a car/house do not.)

> **66**
>
> *I am on Youth Allowance and Rent Assistance through Centrelink. The process was mostly straightforward, but my dad helped me figure it out. Although recently I discovered they messed up my change of address and now I have to call them. Not excited about that.*
>
> Amelie, 18
> – 10 years with a missionary organisation

Receiving payments

Full-time study in this context usually means a 75% course load. Four courses is generally a full study load, so three courses is enough to qualify for full-time study support. Students also often qualify for a one-off payment at the beginning of the school year to help cover the cost of textbooks and other supplies.

None of these payments provide enough to live on comfortably but they can be very helpful support, especially when studying, starting out, or if you suddenly find yourself between jobs.

With all forms of Centrelink payment, your payments begin from the date of your application. It often takes weeks for an application to be processed, in which case you will be back-paid for the time that the application was in process. While receiving Centrelink payments, you must report your income (from any source, including gifts) every two weeks, even if you had no income.

Centrelink payments are only valid while you are present in Australia. If you leave Australia for any reason, including to visit family, your payments will stop until you return. If you know you will be leaving the country (such as on holiday), it is helpful to let Centrelink know ahead of time, giving them your exit date and planned re-entry date. If you leave Australia on a trip that is part of a course of study, ask for a waiver letter from your university to give to Centrelink. The amount of time you are out of the country for study purposes should not affect your Centrelink payment.

While Centrelink is linked to passport control and should automatically stop/restart payments, giving notice shows you are aware of your payment limits. It is important to double-check that your payment restarts when you return! When I (Tanya) travelled overseas while receiving Austudy payments, I was sent messages telling me my payments had stopped, but not that they had restarted. On the other hand, friends recently told me their payments did not stop when they left the country, despite notifying Centrelink they were moving away. They are placing the payments in a separate account, expecting to be asked to return the money at some point in the future.

66

I applied for Austudy when I was a student. There were a few hiccups that delayed the start of payments and I wasn't able to retrospectively receive money either. I think the staff have a difficult time with some customers so I don't blame them, but often they were not very helpful – they would just say you have to do such and such a thing online, or put us on the phone (I suppose the staff in the offices in town don't have the authority to do certain things). The worst blunder was not realising I was receiving money as a loan I did not apply for. The bank statement just said Centrelink so I assumed it was part of my Austudy payments. Many months later I logged in to the ATO to do my

taxes and saw that it showed I owed money on a loan I never applied for – that was quite a shock.
Johnny, 36
– 18 years for family reasons

Centrelink can be very confusing to navigate, so don't be afraid to ask for help! Talking with someone who recently interacted with Centrelink can give you useful tips. The online portal is generally helpful, and when you do get through on the phone, the staff are usually kind. Try to stay calm, and don't be afraid to ask questions if you are unsure. You can also visit a Centrelink shopfront in person, though this is usually not the most time-effective way of doing things unless there is a task that must be done in person.

Another thing to keep in mind if you are receiving Centrelink benefits is tax obligations. If both Centrelink and the ATO (Australian Tax Office) are connected to your myGov account, the information about your Centrelink payments should be automatically added to your tax filing. This has worked well for me (Tanya) in the past. You will want to check the numbers, however, as you are the one liable if something goes wrong.

"
Centrelink and the tax office do not work well together, so I have had many different issues with being able to pay my tax.
Milly, 21
– 10 years for family reasons

To learn more about Centrelink outside of the myGov portal, go to servicesaustralia.gov.au

Tertiary Education

When living overseas, especially if attending international schools, TCKs often hear about only one option for tertiary education: university. There are in fact many options for tertiary studies, and depending on what path you want to take in life, university might not be the best path to get you where you want to go. All recognised tertiary study options (such as those we have outlined below) qualify for financial support through Centrelink, such as Youth Allowance.

Most Australian TCKs are aware that there are government subsidies for university education, through the FEE-HELP program (which we discuss next). The Australian government also subsidises tertiary education in other ways. For general information about tertiary study and careers after high schools, visit yourcareer.gov.au

TAFE (Technical and Further Education)
TAFE is a service that provides education after high school in vocational areas such as accounting, aged care, beauty, business, counselling, design, disability services, hospitality, IT, marketing, real estate, and more. Each state offers their own system, sometimes under different names. TAFE focuses on specific skills needed in the workplace, so each course of study is connected with a specific job. For example, a certificate in childcare teaches all the skills needed to work in childcare, and the resulting certification is recognised across the country.

The Australian government subsidises TAFE courses according to how much need the community has for workers in that field. These subsidies take the place of FEE-HELP loans, meaning that TAFE graduates have only their upfront course costs to pay – and no loan to pay back. Some courses are more heavily subsidised than others, including certain courses that are available fee-free. These places are targeted to young people between the ages of 17-24. If you are eligible, you can study for a diploma, certificate, or short course without a fee. Government incentives and student programs may differ from state to state. Learn more at tafecourses.com.au

Trade Apprenticeships
The Australian Apprenticeships program connects learners directly with workplaces, enabling you to work (and get paid) while you study. The government offers financial support both to the apprentice (to help them get started in their profession) and to the workplace (to incentivise them to take on the work of teaching someone new to the profession). Most apprenticeships include both time at TAFE to learn aspects of the profession, as well as hands-on experience on the job site. Apprenticeship jobs include trades (plumbers, electricians, carpenters, mechanics), food service (chefs, bakers, butchers), some medical fields (vets, nursing, ambulance officers), and much more! Learn more about the apprentice program at apprenticeships.gov.au

Australian Defence Force (ADF)

The Australian Defence Force (ADF) offers fully-funded tertiary training options to those who sign up to a term in the military (generally around nine years). This leads to a role as an officer in the Army, Navy, or Air Force; your term of military service commences immediately after you are appointed. Areas of study available through the ADF include aviation, business management, and engineering; courses of study are based in NSW or Canberra. My (Kath's) cousin secured an engineering education through the Navy, followed by a term of service. If you decide it's not for you, you can leave any time in the first or second year of your studies without any obligation or repayments. Learn more at adfcareers.gov.au

University

If you are looking into attending university for tertiary education, information for attending Australian universities, including admissions criteria and the application process, can be found at the Universities Admission Centre website. This website has everything you need to know about applying to attend an Australian university: uac.edu.au

FEE-HELP

One of the things I (Kath) never knew until I went overseas is the financial stress some young people and their families go through when applying for university. They often worry about how they are going to pay, and they look for scholarships to help with otherwise unmanageable fees. This surprised me; in Australia the process of applying to and paying for university is much simpler and less stressful. 81% of our cohort had attended university in Australia through the local system. 94% of our cohort knew what FEE-HELP was, and 70% had used it.

This high rate of university attendance among our cohort (compared to the general population) is in line with previous studies into higher education among Third Culture Kids. As I (Tanya) wrote in my book *Misunderstood*, "Statistics gathered by Denise Bonebright (*HRD challenges and opportunities*) and Ann Cottrell (*Military Brats and Other Global Nomads*) show 95% of TCKs receive at least some tertiary education, and nearly a third attain an advanced degree. In comparison, 60% of high school graduates in the US enrolled in university in 2001, and 20-30% of adults in Western countries have university degrees."

FEE-HELP (previously known as HECS – Higher Education Contribution Scheme) is a system of government loans available to Australian citizens enrolled in registered Australian tertiary institutions. Tertiary study includes but is not limited to university study. It also encompasses technical schools such as TAFE and any registered institution providing training in skilled labour. There are many great tertiary training avenues outside the university-specific pathway that can lead to well-paid professions.

FEE-HELP loans directly pay tuition costs to the institution and are repaid as automatic taxes once the individual earns enough to qualify for repayment. (You may also voluntarily repay your FEE-HELP loan faster than required.) 16% of our cohort had completely paid off a FEE-HELP loan; 23% were in the process of paying off a FEE-HELP loan. It is important to note that FEE-HELP loan repayments have become more difficult with interest rate rises; these debts were originally interest free, but are now indexed – and often rise higher than salaries.

Learn more about FEE-HELP at studyassist.gov.au/help-loans/fee-help

Getting FEE-HELP

Most Australian tertiary students will qualify for FEE-HELP. You must be an Australian citizen enrolled in an eligible course at a registered institution before that institution's census date. During the enrolment process, your institution will discuss payment with you, including assessment of your FEE-HELP eligibility. Assuming you are eligible, they should show you how to sign up for your FEE-HELP loan as part of the enrolment process. Some universities provide better support than others, though! If in doubt, do not be shy about visiting student services to find someone who can answer your questions.

66
Upon enrolment you are asked how you would like to pay for your fees and once you click that you would like to defer your payment with FEE-HELP, it simply keeps track of what you owe. Once you begin earning enough, you will start paying it off. I am paying my amenities fees upfront each semester.
Danielle, 19
– 11 years with a missionary organisation

FEE-HELP only pays your tuition; other costs, such as accommodation, textbooks, and service fees, will be up to you. This is where Austudy often helps.

It is not mandatory to take out a FEE-HELP loan, and there are lifetime limits to how much you can take out in loans. My (Tanya's) parents paid for my undergraduate degree outright, which meant a 25% discount on the posted rate and nothing to pay back. When I did my master's degree a decade later, I was able to get a FEE-HELP loan to cover the full cost of my tuition.

66

I received FEE-HELP on multiple degrees over 20 years or so. It was essential to being able to engage in tertiary education.
Derek, 45
– 10 years with a missionary organisation

Chapter 11:

Services Available to You as an Australian Citizen Overseas

Smartraveller

The first service for Australians outside Australia to be aware of is Smartraveller. In the past, Australians leaving Australia (whether short or long term) were asked to register their details in order to receive important communications. This changed during the COVID-19 pandemic. There are no longer general registrations. Instead, the Australian government opens specific registrations for regions in crisis. For example, in April 2023 a registration was opened for Australians living in Sudan due to the war that broke out there.

When the COVID-19 pandemic began in 2020, I (Tanya) was living outside Australia and registered with Smartraveller. This meant I received the warning email from the Australian government a week before the Australian border shut. (Although they also told us to stay where we were if we had a safe place to live and access to healthcare – no one predicted the two years that followed!)

The Smartraveller service now exists as an optional newsletter sign up. You can choose to receive updates on any/all countries/regions of interest to you, whether or not you are there at the moment. These email updates come from the Australian government, with advice for Australian citizens living in or planning to travel to these places. When this change took place during the pandemic, I (Tanya) chose to receive a daily email bulletin of all notices worldwide, which I continue to receive. I usually skim through to see if there is anything I want to know more about. The notices include changed border requirements, local emergencies, travel advisories, and so on.

We recommend signing up for a Smartraveller newsletter for any country outside Australia you are living in, travelling in, or planning to travel to in the next few months. The Smartraveller website also has information and advice about all sorts of topics of interest to Australians travelling and/or living outside Australia. Learn more about these services (and more) at smartraveller.gov.au

> **"**
> *Smartraveller can be helpful in a place you're unsure about.*
> Olivia, 23
> – 10 years with a missionary organisation

> **"**
> *Smartraveller is of value and I would recommend it. Behavioural and security aspects can be important to know, especially if visiting a new context.*
> David, 61
> – 6 years in aid and development

Consular services

Another helpful resource is your local Australian embassy, high commission, or consulate. 43% of our cohort visited an Australian embassy at least once as a child; 6% visited often. 48% of those who lived overseas as adults said they had visited an Australian embassy at least once, but only 2% visited often. Depending on where you live, the closest embassy might be in another city or even another country. Wherever you live and whenever you travel, it is always good to know where the closest Australian consular assistance can be found and how to make contact. If you hold dual citizenship, learn the closest assistance for each of your passport countries. (Note that Australian embassies will not assist dual citizens in the country of their other citizenship.)

> **"**
> *My main interaction with the embassy was the Anzac Day* dawn service and free breakfast, which I highly recommend.*
> Katie, 24
> – 14 years with a missionary organisation

"
I always remember the Australian Embassy closing while I was in Peru when the situation became dire. We then came under the Canadian Embassy. While the Australian Embassy existed, they held really nice gatherings that my parents attended.
Sally, 52
– 7 years with a missionary organisation

"
I've visited the Australian consulates in my country many times – for issuing passports, citizenship certificates for my children, notarising documents, etc. The only hassle usually is the travel distance, going to the capital city.
Marco, 64
– 11 years with a missionary organisation, 5 years with the ADF

"
My birth certificate is from an Australian consulate. In one country, we would often visit the high commission to use the pool there.
Brush, 70
– 12 years with a missionary organisation

There are many reasons for being aware of, and making use of, consular services. First up, consular staff are there when things go wrong. If your passport is stolen, you are arrested or questioned by police, or an Australian family member dies abroad, consular staff can help you. The Consular Services Charter (which can be found at smartraveller. gov.au) outlines all the services Australian consular staff can provide to Australians overseas, and the limits of these services. It is well worth the time for every Australian who travels or lives overseas to read this document and understand what your government can and cannot do for you, and what you are expected to do for yourself when you travel.

A few of these services are for normal life – not just emergencies. We want to point out a few that are important to be aware of. Keep in mind that not all embassies and consulates can provide the same services. You always need to check with your local outpost to see what they offer rather than assuming.

1. **Passports**
   Australian embassies and consulates can issue Australian passports. This means you can get your passport renewed without having to travel back to Australia. Ten years ago, I (Tanya) had my passport renewed at the Australian Embassy in Beijing. (More on this in the next section.)

   66
   I visited the Australian Embassy in London to get a new passport.
   Shellie, 54
   – 1 year with the ADF

2. **Notary services**
   Embassies can also provide notary services when you need an Australian document officially witnessed. There is a fee for this but when you have piles of paperwork to do, it can be a lifesaver! I (Tanya) had an Australia police check sent from Australia to China for a work visa without getting it notarised in Australia first – disaster! But I was able to take it to the Australian Embassy in Beijing and get it notarised there, which saved me a lot of time and even money in the long run.

3. **Voting**
   Another consular service Australia provides is the opportunity to vote (see *Chapter 9*). Voting is an important way for Australian citizens to have a voice in our government. We both believe this is particularly important for Australians overseas, who are affected by the decisions of our government but often have less of a voice in these matters. You are not required to vote while living outside Australia, but it is an opportunity – a privilege – worth taking advantage of. The treatment of Australians outside Australia during the COVID-19 pandemic showed how important it is that this portion of the Australian population have a voice in how Australia makes decisions on behalf of its citizens.

   66
   The right to vote is such a privilege and one that should be taken seriously. Look around the world at all the countries where it's so dangerous to vote – or impossible.
   Shellie, 54
   – 1 year with the ADF

Passports overseas

Your passport is an essential bit of paperwork when you travel outside Australia. In some countries you may even be required to carry it with you wherever you go. In many countries you will be required to present your passport when making almost any official transaction: setting up a bank account, renting an apartment, or getting a job. In some countries you may be able to obtain a local ID card that you can use instead, but not always. In any case, you will certainly need your passport to travel.

The biggest difference when renewing your passport overseas is that there is no mail-in option. This option exists in Australia because Australia Post staff can witness your identity upon receiving your mail-in application. Outside Australia, you must go to the embassy/consulate in person to apply for your new passport. If you live far from your embassy and/or are renewing a child's passport, the process can get complicated quickly.

Passport renewal usually takes several weeks, no matter where in the world you are. In some places, a rush service may be possible. Emergency passports can be issued in special circumstances; they are only valid for one year and do not have a chip, which means they cannot be used everywhere. Provisional travel documents can sometimes be provided by an embassy/consulate, which may be a solution while waiting for a passport to be ready.

You need six months' validity on your passport to get a visa to most countries, so make sure you keep an eye on that. My (Tanya's) rule of thumb is to make a renewal plan when I have one year of validity left on my passport. First, decide where you will renew your passport. You have to be in that place long enough to lodge your passport renewal and get the new passport back. If your closest embassy is far away from where you usually live and work, this might be a problem. If it is a different city in the same country, you may be able to travel on a local ID. If your closest consulate is in a different country, you may need another plan. Asking your embassy about provisional travel documents might be part of that plan. Taking advantage of a trip to Australia that takes place even a year before your passport expires might be a better solution.

If you do renew your passport overseas, you will need to check the process where you will renew – it is a bit different everywhere. You will likely need to fill out forms online and print them to bring in. You will need passport photos taken according to Australian requirements, which may be different to passport photo requirements in that country. When I (Tanya) renewed my passport in China, the passport photos I brought were rejected. I was directed to a photo studio a 15-minute walk away which understood how to take photos for Australian passports.

> **"**
> *I've renewed my passport from Canada. At first, the process seemed very intimidating because you have to have an in-person interview at a local embassy or consulate – and my nearest one was at least three hours' drive away. However, I discovered that there are consulate outreaches, where officials travel to major cities on certain dates to do passport interviews, which made them much more accessible. I only had to drive 1.5 hours. Besides that, the actual process was pretty simple, and just involved filling out forms and taking photos, like any passport renewal. The passport photos had different specifications to Canadian passport photos, so we had to find a local photographer who takes pictures for international passports – we couldn't just walk into a Walmart or something. I highly recommend staying on top of passport renewals because applying for a new Australian passport from overseas sounds intimidating.*
> Lyndall, 30
> – 5 years for family reasons

Another note on passports specifically for dual citizens: Australia expects all dual nationals to enter and exit Australia on their Australian passports. Once you leave Australia, you are free to use your other passport to enter the country you are heading to. This means that if you/your child are granted citizenship while living outside Australia, it is important to apply for a passport!

Chapter 12:

Family and Paperwork

One of the realities of international living is that you are more likely to have an international life and family. You are more likely to marry someone of a different nationality, like I (Tanya) did. You are more likely to have children outside Australia, or adopt children in/from other countries. You are more likely to raise children with multilayered heritage and identity. In this section, we look at some of the consequences of these decisions, so you can plan ahead. The goal of this section is not a warning, not to say "don't do this hard thing!" but rather to arm you with knowledge so that whatever happens in your life, you have the tools you need to smooth out the bumps.

Marriage

Let's start with marriage. If you marry outside Australia, or marry someone who is not an Australian, there are a few things to keep in mind. I (Tanya) had lived outside Australia for so long and had so many friends in mixed-nationality marriages by the time I got engaged to my American husband that I had already done most of the research on the list below – to work out the best way forward for us, legally speaking. Even before we got serious, I took note of this kind of legal nonsense, knowing it would be part of our lives forever if we eventually got married. When I committed to him, I committed to him no matter what our governments threw at us. (And it's a good thing I did, as dealing with three separate government bureaucracies during the COVID-19 pandemic has kept us living apart for over three years!)

When you are looking at getting married to a non-Australian, or to an Australian outside Australia, first think about how to ensure your marriage is legal. You want it to be legally recognised in Australia, in your partner's country, and in the country (or countries) in which you live. One of the three is not going to be enough! Especially when you think long term. Something that isn't a problem now could pose a problem in the future.

66
I married another TCK. She was from the UK; our wedding was in Australia. I had to work through the legal issues here in Australia after I proposed.
David, 61
– 6 years in aid and development

Getting married outside Australia

If you get married outside Australia, you may need to provide documentation to that country's government that you are free to marry. This may include a Certificate of No Impediment to Marriage (CNI); this can be issued by DFAT in Australia, but depending on where you are getting married, it may need to be issued by the Australian embassy there.

66
I married overseas, but as a dual citizen of the country where I got married, it wasn't an overly complicated process.
Tamar, 50
– 18 years in the business sector

66
I was married in Scotland (my ex-husband's country) because we were living in London at the time and really, who could go past getting married in a castle! But also because there was no way his family could have afforded to travel to Australia, whereas my family could travel to Scotland. We had a second reception in Australia three months later with all my family and friends.
Shellie, 54
– 1 year with the ADF

You may also need a Single Status Certificate, No Record Result (another name for the CNI), and original birth certificate; if you were born in Australia, you can get these from the Registry of Births, Deaths and Marriages in the state or territory where you were born. If you have been previously married, you may need to show your divorce papers or the death certificate of your late spouse.

While you will not need to register your marriage with the Australian government in order for it to be recognised, other countries may require registration of an overseas marriage. Depending on your partner's nationality, or the country in which you live, marrying outside Australia may be easier for you.

Legal recognition of marriages outside Australia

If your marriage was legal under the laws of the land where the marriage took place *and* fits the description of a legal marriage in Australia, it will be recognised in Australia. Keep in mind that Australian-authorised wedding celebrants cannot legally officiate a wedding outside Australia. Some of the main reasons an overseas marriage will not be recognised as legal by Australia is if either party was already married, if either were under the age of 16 while they or the other party was an Australian resident, or if any fraud or duress took place.

You are *not* required to register an overseas marriage with an Australian embassy, and it cannot be registered as an Australian marriage, but it will be recognised by Australia as a legal marriage. That said, marriage certificates will not necessarily be immediately recognised on sight. Depending on the country, it will need to be officially translated and notarised.

One thing a foreign marriage certificate will not do in Australia is serve as proof for a change of name. If you wish to change your name when you marry overseas, you will have to apply for your name change separately (and pay a fee).

Visa/residency through marriage

If you are interested in getting a visa or residency/citizenship for yourself or your partner on account of your marriage, again, look up the rules *before* tying the knot! Many people assume that marriage automatically gains you access to your partner's country, but this is rarely the case.

An Australian citizen engaged or married to a non-citizen can apply for a fiancé(e) or spouse visa for them to enter Australia. Once they have entered Australia on that visa, they can apply for permanent residence based on their marriage. There is a *lot* of money and paperwork before getting to that point, however.

Australia is one of the most (if not the most) expensive places in the world to get residency as the spouse of a citizen. As of 2023, the cost is around $8,000. In addition to the financial cost, you will need to submit paperwork demonstrating that your relationship is truly committed, not just romantically but socially, financially, and as a household. This might include joint ownership of assets, shared domestic responsibilities, and knowledge of the relationship by others in your lives.

> **"**
> *We got permanent residency for my husband (from Puerto Rico, a US citizen). It was one of the most stressful things I've done. Hours of painstakingly building a portfolio of evidence to prove your relationship is genuine, committed, and ongoing. Ticking all the boxes, making sure not to miss anything. The huge cost involved as well. I researched online, reading the government websites to make sure we were doing it right. Called immigration a few times. Had my sister call and confirm for me once too. In the end we found out we could get married while he was on a visa waiver tourist visa and then change our Prospective Marriage Visa to a Spouse/Defacto Visa with no charge to make the change so long as we did it in the time frame. We had to apply for a prospective one first because we didn't have evidence of being a spouse. Once we got married we got the marriage certificate and made the visa change request. He then had to leave Australia every three months (he visited PNG and we holidayed in NZ for these and re-entered Australia after one to two weeks) a couple times until his temporary spouse visa got approved. It was then just a waiting process for that to become a permanent residency.*
> Anna, 29
> – 16 years with a missionary organisation

A similar process is required by many other countries. You may or may not be able to live in the country where you married, or in the passport country of your partner, after marriage. If you marry on a tourist visa, you might not be able to apply to stay on unless you can prove you had no intention of marrying when you arrived in the country. Every country has different rules, and it is impossible to predict what they will be without looking it up. These rules also tend to change frequently, so do not go by what worked for someone else in the past.

> **"**
> *I got a US Green Card – which was not as easy as people think! People think 'Oh, you just get married and you get one' but when I got my green card my husband had to have $60,000 in a bank account in case I was to fall back on welfare. We were 21 – he didn't have $60,000! So his mother was my financial supporter. Then we had to prove his parents' and his grandparents' citizenship. The paperwork was just one part of the horrible experience.*
> Lisa, 45
> – 17 years in the business sector

Do your research

The common thread through all of this: do your research before planning a wedding, so you can make the best choice for your unique situation.

I (Tanya) chose to legally marry in the USA (my husband's country) because my research told me it was the simplest solution for us. Australia would recognise my American marriage certificate without any other documentation required, and having a US marriage certificate would make any future paperwork on the US side simpler.

I have had many friends who wanted to marry in China, where they and their partner lived and met, but it is literally impossible for partners from different countries (where neither is Chinese) to legally marry there. So in these cases they had a legal civil paper-signing elsewhere and a public (though not legally binding) ceremony at home in Beijing.

One of my close friends chose to hire a small agency in Thailand to conduct a civil ceremony and do all the paperwork to ensure their marriage was legally recognised by both partners' countries – even though neither of them were from, or lived in, Thailand. Then they had a church wedding in the country where they wanted to celebrate with their friends and family, without having to worry about the legalities.

The bottom line is that there are lots of possibilities and options. When considering marriage to a non-Australian, or outside Australia, go to the Smartraveller website to read the latest information about marriage law for Australians, and check the Australian Embassy page for the countries relevant to your location and your partner's country to find out what else might be applicable to your situation.

> **"**
> *I was quite happy with my Australian citizenship and my US Green Card, even though I really wanted to vote. But then we adopted our son. Our adoption attorney asked when I would be applying for my US citizenship. I replied, 'I don't need to be a citizen of the United States to be his mother.' She said to me, 'You never know. Someone could change immigration law and you could get separated from your family.' I realised then there's no guarantee, so I applied for my citizenship the next day.*
> Lisa, 45
> – 17 years in the business sector

Global families

Next, we come to children. Did you know that children born to two Australian citizens outside Australia are not automatically Australian citizens? Did you know that not all countries give children citizenship according to *jus soli* (by being born there) – including Australia? This means that if you are living overseas, or have a partner with a different citizenship/heritage, it is important to think well in advance about citizenship options for children you might have.

Obtaining Australian citizenship for your child

Australia followed *jus soli* until August 20th, 1986. Anyone born on Australian soil before this date was automatically an Australian citizen. Since then, someone born in Australia must have at least one parent who is an Australian citizen or resident to qualify for Australian citizenship. A child born in Australia to non-Australian parents can usually apply for citizenship if they live in Australia for 10 years following their birth, or after at least four years holding permanent residency and passing an English proficiency test.

Children adopted by Australian parents living in Australia are treated as natural-born children and automatically granted Australian citizenship. Citizenship is not automatically granted to children adopted by

Australian parents overseas, but they may apply for it. This can be a complicated – and expensive – process, especially if the adoption was processed by a non-Australian agency. I know several families with dual citizenship/residency who began the process of getting Australian citizenship for their children born and adopted overseas, but eventually gave up. Another such family is moving ahead despite the prohibitive costs and difficult timing requirements, to ensure their children have legal access to the country in which they visit their grandparents and cousins.

Children born to Australian citizens outside Australia (including through an international surrogacy agreement) can receive citizenship by descent, but this is not automatic – it must be applied for. From birth to the age of 18, a parent or legal guardian may apply on a child's behalf; from age 15–25, an individual may apply on their own behalf.

"
My birth certificate is from Nepal; it does not look official, the date uses the Nepali calendar, but does have a regular calendar date written as well. There was concern it would not be accepted as a legal document. I have not had any difficulties as I also have Australian citizenship by descent paperwork which is used more often than my birth certificate. Despite concerns that it would be difficult to apply for Australian passports or any other documentation/licences, this has not been the case.
Josie, 35
– 7 years with a missionary organisation

"
My sister has had trouble at different times with documents due to being born overseas. She let her passport lapse during Covid and has vowed never to let it happen again. Having your birth registered through an embassy before the world went digital makes it hard to prove your identity.
Alice, 52
– 8 years with DFAT

"

My son was born in the UK. My wife and I organised Australian citizenship there quite easily after his birth.
David, 61
– 6 years in aid and development

A child eligible for citizenship by descent or citizenship by adoption but who has not yet received it is allowed to travel to Australia on a non-Australian passport with an Australian visa. Once a child has Australian citizenship, they must travel into and out of Australia on an Australian passport. This means that if you apply for Australian citizenship for your child and plan to travel internationally, it is vital that you also get them an Australian passport. (They will no longer be able to use any other passport/s to travel into/out of Australia.)

The rules surrounding citizenship change, including whether/how a citizen by descent can pass Australian citizenship onto their own child, and whether/how a citizen by descent can attain citizenship without restriction. As with everything, do some research into your own situation to work out the best solution for your family.

The website for all citizenship applications (including applying on behalf of your child) is immi.homeaffairs.gov.au

Other citizenship(s) for your child

If your partner has a different citizenship to you, if either of you has or qualifies for dual citizenship, or if your child is born outside Australia, look into all the citizenship possibilities open to your child. Find out which citizenships, if any, they qualify for.

Some countries have citizenship possibilities that 'expire' – that must be applied for within a certain time frame, or by a certain age. Do your research and know your options. If you do not get a certain citizenship for your child, let it be by choice, and not because you missed a deadline.

If your child does qualify for another citizenship, take time to investigate and understand the responsibilities of citizenship there. Many countries have required duties, such as national military service, that you would commit your child to by applying for citizenship on their behalf.

Learn whether the other country allows for dual citizenship, as Australia does. Will your child be forced to choose between passports? Will you be okay if they do not choose to share your citizenship? Once you give them two passports that they will have to choose between one day, you give them the freedom to make their own decision – even if it is not the decision you might expect, or wish.

Perhaps you will choose a situation that means your child does not automatically get Australian citizenship, and you choose not to apply for it on their behalf. If so, make sure you keep up with the rules of citizenship by descent so that when they are old enough to apply on their own, you can support them well should they make that choice.

Part of living an international life is opening the world to children. Do your best to support whatever choices your child makes – whether it is to give up a country you love or to choose a country you did not choose for them.

> **"**
> *Our five-year-old has a really strong family identity, even though he hasn't seen his American family for two years now. When you ask him who his family is he lists all of them, the ones here and the ones there. I love that because it reminds me of when I was growing up; I had a strong sense of family – this is my family even though we're in different countries. He'll proudly tell you he's American and Australian, and he doesn't think it's fair that Mummy's only Australian.*
> Jean, 33
> – 18 years with a missionary organisation

Giving birth outside Australia

There are two things to keep in mind here: healthcare and citizenship. When it comes to maternal and obstetric healthcare, Australia citizens receive great care for free through Medicare (see *Chapter 10*). Children also receive free vaccinations. My (Tanya's) sisters chose the Australia public system for their children's births despite having access to private healthcare. If money or healthcare outcomes are concerns where you are living, returning to Australia for a period of time before and after your child's birth may be a good choice for your family. This may also be helpful in regards to citizenship as if either you or your partner is an Australian citizen, your child will have automatic Australian citizenship.

> **"**
> *My mother made the decision to return to Australia to give birth to me for her own medical safety due to a pre-existing condition and to ensure that I didn't have trouble with documents as an adult. Other families who gave birth in Southeast Asia struggled with Australian birth certificates for their children and often there were errors that took many months to rectify. My mother returning to Australia for a couple of months while my dad continued working overseas means that as an adult I have no issues with passports and anything else that requires extra documentation when you're born overseas.*
> Rosie, 25
> – 6 years with DFAT

If you are comfortable with your healthcare options and choose to give birth outside Australia, the next thing to look into is whether the country grants citizenship on a *jus soli* basis. That is, will being born there make your child a citizen of the country? If so, make sure you are aware of the responsibilities of citizenship there and what you are committing your child to by choosing to give birth to them there.

If the country does *not* grant *jus soli* citizenship, make sure you have a plan to get your child legal status soon after they are born. This generally involves three steps:

1. Citizenship by descent
2. Passport
3. Visa

You will also need to check the grace period the country you are in allows for newborns to get through these steps and gain a legal visa – to make sure your child is not an illegal alien! We strongly recommend that you acquire all the requisite forms and fill in as much as possible before the birth so that after your child has arrived, all you have to do is fill in their name, date of birth, and anything else relevant to the birth. Then submit and get the process going as quickly as possible!

"
Both of my children were born overseas, and there were no issues getting them Australian citizenship, and subsequently, passports."
Tamar, 50
– 18 years in the business sector

Conclusion:

Australia is Complex – and Worth it

Australian citizenship comes with rights and responsibilities – benefits available to you and ways to contribute. There are mainstream Australian cultural norms, and understanding these helps you connect with others in Australia. But there are also hundreds of ways to be Australian.

86% of our cohort said they were Australian, though half of those said it was only a small part of their identity. 12% said that while they were legally Australian, they didn't feel Australian. When we asked our cohort what their Australian citizenship meant to them, practical answers tended to resonate most strongly. And that's okay!

- 78% = A passport I can travel on
- 78% = Access to Australia
- 73% = Access to Australian services
- 66% = Connection to Australian friends/family
- 59% = A home base
- 57% = Part of who I am
- 40% = My family's heritage

You get to choose what being Australian means to you. The things you love and are proud of about Australia may be very different to what others love and are proud of. The things you dislike or are even ashamed of may be very different as well. Those differences don't make you – or them – any more or less Australian. You are not a 'bad' Australian for your differences. Your differences can actually make you an asset to Australia!

"
I'm an Australian citizen, and I am not a foreigner to Australian culture, I just have other elements of cultural background as well. If I do or say or think things that other Australians think are 'un-Australian', too bad. I am Australian and I am a member of this community and I have a right to engage with this culture, including criticising it and supporting efforts to change it. I don't have that right in other cultures. I'm not a part of them, and I don't understand them well enough to criticise. I need to approach

other cultures humbly. I need to approach my fellow Australians humbly too, but I think I have a right to criticise and a right to have an opinion about how the culture should grow and change. I do feel like a 'bad Australian' when it comes to the treatment of Indigenous people and asylum seekers. Not that I am bad at being Australian, but that Australia is being bad and I am a part of it.
Katie, 24
– 14 years with a missionary organisation

"
Before when people would challenge me on certain things – for example, our refugee policies – I was ashamed and didn't want to have anything to do with it. Now I defend my country. Yes, we're doing a terrible job on this, but this is my country and I am seeking to make it a better place. I am emotionally involved and I'm working to make my home a better place. This is a significant shift: I can still see the same problems but now I am included within that sphere, so I am going to work for change within this space that I am part of and am included in.
Nathan, 28
– 5 years with a missionary organisation

"
I never feel like a 'bad Australian' because I try to speak up on inequalities, support inclusion initiatives, and am ashamed by our treatment of refugees and asylum seekers.
Hurley, 64
– 3 years with the ADF

Whatever you do, don't write off *all* Australians. Take your time, get to know more people, and practise some grace and kindness towards yourself and others. You'll find your people eventually. You can create your own sense of home in this country, in a way that feels like home to *you*.

"
I love Australia. No matter where I go, I still get excited to touch down and step off the plane and smell the eucalyptus in the air.
Elaine, 26
– 3 years with a missionary organisation

"
I feel like a 'real Australian' when I get to go through the Australian passport holder channel at immigration! Also when I vote, when I participate in civic life, and when Australia is positively portrayed in international media.
Marco, 64
– 11 years with a missionary organisation, 5 years with the ADF

One last thing to keep in mind: it's okay if Australia doesn't feel like home. It's okay to love and miss another place. It's okay to have more than one home! Loving two places is not a betrayal of either one. We want you to have the most positive experience you can, to have your own unique journey that results in you feeling at home in your own skin, wherever you live. That means owning the truths of your life: of who you are, where you live, where your heart's home/s are – and that the answers to these questions can change over time.

"
Initially after moving back, I was adamant I would not like Australia. I was too attached to my previous country and felt like the only way I could hold on to my life there was to continue perceiving it as my home. I was mad at how hard it was to adjust to Australia and how difficult it was to feel settled. However, making friends and the feeling of being out of place was hard enough already without at least accepting that I live here now. While Australia still doesn't feel home to me, I know the place where I used to live isn't entirely home. Now I accept that I live here and that there are good things about Australia, but I will always have more love and fond memories of my overseas country.
Danielle, 19
– 11 years with a missionary organisation

> **"**
> *Don't shut yourself off from relationships with Australians who have spent their whole lives here. They can be really rich relationships and you can learn from them. Don't let the richness of your wonderful TCK experience cut you off from what Australian people might teach you. Don't let the feelings of not fitting in or the perspective you have – where you can see things that are wrong with Australian culture – make you bitter or overly critical. Be open to what you can learn.*
> Lucy, 38
> – 9 years with a missionary organisation

Developing a positive relationship with your passport country (or countries) isn't always easy. It is worth it, though. Working at feeling comfortable and at home in your passport country is an investment that pays off. It allows you to come home any time, whatever happens in the world. It allows you to inhabit your citizenship, making it more than a piece of paper.

We are glad to share this country – and this journey – with you.

Tanya and Kath
Canberra/Adelaide
September 2023

Resources

Glossary of Australian vocabulary

There are lots of good lists of Aussie slang online, but we thought we'd add a list of our own favourites (and ones that tripped us or our friends up) for you here, along with all the slang and Aussie terms found in the rest of the book. Keep in mind that slang is generally only used in casual speech – but that could still be with colleagues around the office!

_____ as: almost any adjective could go here (e.g. busy as, awesome as, tired as). It's an intensifier, like adding "extremely" on the front.

ABC: Australian Broadcasting Corporation, the national broadcaster of Australia.

AFL: Australian Football League (also known as Aussie Rules).

Aggro: aggressive.

Akubras: most well-known brand of Australian bush hat, typically wide-brimmed and made of felted rabbit fur.

Anglo: short for 'Anglo-Saxon', a term commonly used in Australia to refer to Caucasians of Western European backgrounds.

ANZAC: Australian and New Zealand Army Corps, the name under which Australian and New Zealand troops fought in World War I.

Anzac biscuits: a biscuit made with oats and golden syrup. The recipe was created in 1915 to send to soldiers fighting overseas in WWI. Also see: **ANZAC**.

Anzac Day: national day of commemoration in Australia and New Zealand for victims of war and for recognition of the role of their armed forces. Takes place on April 25th every year, in memory of the first major military action fought by Australian and New Zealand forces, at Gallipoli in Turkey, where the Allied troops landed at dawn on April 25th in a place now known as Anzac Cove. Also see: **ANZAC**.

Arvo: afternoon.

Australia Day: Australia's national day on the 26th of January. Australia became a nation on January 1st 1901, and different states celebrated Australia on different days over time until the 1990s when January 26th was made a federal holiday. This date marks the first white settlement of the continent, marked by Indigenous Australians for many decades as a Day of Mourning, and more recently as Invasion Day.

Avo: avocado.

Bag out: to criticise someone.

Barrack: to cheer for a sporting team. See also: **Go for**.

Bathers: swimsuit. See also: **Cossie**, **Swimmers**, **Togs**.

Bikkie: biscuit (cookie). Also spelled: bicky.

Bloody: an adjective of emphasis, especially for expressing shock or anger.

Bludger: a lazy person.

Bogan: an uncouth, unrefined, or uncultured person, generally perceived to be of low social status. Stereotypically wears a flannel shirt and tight jeans and has their hair cut in a mullet.

Boonies/Boondocks, the: far away area, the outskirts of town, etc.

Bottle-o: liquor store.

Brekkie/Brekky: breakfast.

Bring a plate: if someone tells you to "bring a plate" to a party, they're not asking for extra tableware. They'd actually like you to bring some food to share.

Budgie smugglers: a pair of men's Speedos (small swimsuit briefs).

Bugger: exclamation of annoyance; an annoying or awkward person/ thing. Also used as a verb for anal sex.

Buggered: tired, broken, or ruined. Also see: **Bugger**.

Bush: The bush is a part of Australia which is unsettled and undeveloped, but not as remote as the Outback.

Bushranger: criminals who operated in Australia in the second half of the 19th century and used the bush to hide and escape after committing a crime. See also: **Bush**.

Bushwalking: hiking or backpacking in the bush. See also: **Bush.**

BYO: Bring Your Own. Unless otherwise specified, refers to alcoholic beverages.

Cab Sav: Cabernet Sauvignon (wine).

Cactus: broken, ruined, too tired to do anything.

Call it a day: finish what you're doing.

Chemist: pharmacy (a drugstore that primarily sells medicines).

Chief Minister: the leader of a territory government (ACT/NT) is called the Chief Minister.

Chips: fries, potato chips (cold) or hot chips.

Choccy bicky: chocolate biscuit.

Chockers: abbreviation of 'chock-a-block,' meaning very full.

Combo: combination.

Convo: conversation.

Cossie: swimsuit. See also: **Bather**, **Swimmers**, **Togs**.

Cricket: a bat and ball sport not entirely unlike baseball; originated in England and played throughout the Commonwealth. Australia loves it partly because we win a lot.

Crocodile Dundee: Crocodile Dundee is a 1986 action-comedy film set in the Australian Outback (and New York City) starring Paul Hogan. It was the first introduction to Australia many people overseas had, and it remains a key ingredient in how international audiences (especially US Americans) regard Australia.

Crocodile Hunter: The Crocodile Hunter is a wildlife documentary television series hosted by Steve Irwin. The show was very popular internationally, especially in the US. See also: **Steve Irwin**.

Cronulla riots: the 2005 Cronulla riots were race riots in Sydney, NSW. They began on December 11th, triggered by an event the previous Sunday when an altercation on Cronulla beach between white Anglo lifeguards and a group of youths of Middle Eastern appearance (referred to as "Lebanese" or the slur "Lebs" by the lifeguards) turned physical. This triggered several nights of violence in Cronulla and nearby suburbs.

Cuppa: a hot beverage (usually tea/coffee).

Damper: a traditional Australian soda bread (made from flour, butter, salt, water and/or milk) cooked over an open fire.

Deadpan: dry humour.

Designated driver: a person who abstains from alcohol at a social gathering so as to be fit (sober) to drive others home.

Devon: sliced processed meat, known by different names in different parts of Australia. See also: **Fritz, Polony**.

Dodgy: poor quality/unreliable/suspicious.

Double demerits: periods of time when demerit points for certain traffic offences are doubled, generally during high-risk periods such as school holidays and public holiday weekends.

Dunny: toilet.

EFTPOS: machine for electronic (card) payments. Stands for Electronic Funds Transfer at Point Of Sale.

Esky: ice cooler.

Fair go: to give someone/something a fair chance; often used as an exclamation indicating that something unfair has been said.

Fairy bread: a treat, usually seen at children's birthday parties, consisting of sliced white bread with a generous spread of butter and hundreds and thousands sprinkled over the top.

First Fleet: the group of 11 ships full of prisoners (and guards) sent from England to colonise the landmass that would eventually be known as Australia. They landed near what is now Sydney in January 1788. See also: **Second Fleet**.

Flat white: coffee with milk or cream (not frothed) – a very common coffee order in Australia.

Fritz: sliced processed meat, known by different names in different parts of Australia. See also: **Devon**, **Polony**.

Full-on: intense/wild.

Gallipoli: the location of Anzac Cove, and a WWI battle that looms large in the Australian and New Zealand consciousness. The legend of Gallipoli, and how Australians remember it, has become a central part of how Australia defines itself as a nation. See also: **ANZAC**.

Garbo: garbage man.

G'day: literally "good day". Simply means 'hello'.

Give someone a bell/buzz/holler/ring: call someone on the phone.

Go for: support a sporting team. "Who do you go for?" See also: **Barrack**.

Gold coin donation: optional donation of $1–$2 (the Australian coins minted in gold rather than silver).

Golden syrup: a thick, amber-coloured inverted sugar syrup composed of sugar, water, and citric acid. Also known as light treacle.

Goon: cheap wine in a bag (usually means red).

Green & gold: the national colours of Australia are green and gold, often worn for sporting events, and derived from the national flower, golden wattle.

Green Ps: badge displayed on a car driven by a driver with a Level 2 Provisional Licence.

Grog: any kind of alcoholic beverage.

Grog run: a trip to go and buy alcohol.

Heaps: a lot or very; e.g. "heaps good" or "heaps of people".

How good is that? a rhetorical question meaning "That's great!"

How's it going? a standard greeting, equivalent to "How are you?"

Hungry Jacks/HJs: the Australian version of Burger King.

Kiwi: a New Zealander (but also a fruit and a bird).

Lamington: an Australian cake made from squares of sponge cake coated in an outer layer of chocolate sauce and rolled in desiccated coconut.

L Plates: badge displayed on a car by a learner driver.

Knock: to criticise something.

Kokoda (WWII): the Kokoda Trail campaign in Papua New Guinea was arguably Australia's most significant campaign of the Second World War.

More Australians died on the Kokoda Trail during the seven months of fighting than during any other campaign in Australia's military history, and the Japanese came closer to Australia than during any other land offensive.

Maccas: McDonald's.

Mambo: an Australian clothing brand popular in the 1990s, famous for crude slogans and cartoons.

Mate: friend.

Mozzie: mosquito.

Munted: broken, ruined, too tired/drunk to do anything.

My shout: if it's your 'shout', then it's your turn to buy everyone drinks, as in a pub. See also: **Pub**, **Shout**.

My treat: used to tell someone that you will pay for something such as a meal for them.

Nah, Yeah: yes. See also: **Yeah, Nah**.

Netball: netball is a ball sport not entirely unlike basketball which is theoretically non-contact and is primarily played by women.

Nothin' doin': I will not do that for you.

No worries: don't worry about it/it's okay/not a problem.

NRL: National Rugby League (the top rugby league competition in Australia, which also includes a team from New Zealand).

Ocker: refers to a broad/rural Australian accent; often thought of as uncouth or uncultivated.

One for the road: a last drink before going home.

On your Ls: means you have a learner driver's licence.

On your Ps: means you have a provisional driver's licence.

Ordinary/average: these two words can keep their literal meaning, or be a mild insult to indicate that something is of poor quality.

Outback: any inland area of Australia that is remote from large centres of population.

Oval: a round grassy area for playing sport, especially cricket and AFL (also known as a 'sports oval').

Pacer: mechanical/refillable pencil.

Pavlova: a dessert claimed by both Australia and New Zealand – baked meringue, covered with a thick layer of whipped cream and topped with sliced fresh fruit (traditionally strawberry, kiwi fruit, passionfruit, and maybe banana, though berries are popular for modern versions).

Petrol: fuel for your car (what Americans call 'gas').

Play it by ear: decide as you go.

P.O. box: a Post Office Box; a locked box at a post office which can be rented as a secure way to receive mail.

P Plates: badge displayed on a car driven by a driver with a provisional licence.

Polony: sliced processed meat, known by different names in different parts of Australia. See also: **Devon, Fritz**.

Pom/Pommie: a Brit. A mildly derogatory term, derived from the acronym P.O.M.E. – Prisoner Of Mother England.

Premier: the leader of a state government is called the Premier.

Prime Minister: the Prime Minister is the leader of the Australian Government.

Pub: an establishment for the sale of drinks (especially alcoholic beverages, with beer being the most commonly ordered), and sometimes also food, to be consumed on the premises.

Queenslanda: Queenslander – someone from Queensland, or a style of wooden house with large verandahs common there.

Rashie: a rashguard, also known as a rash vest. An athletic shirt made of spandex and nylon or polyester. It provides sun protection and is commonly worn while enjoying water sports.

RBTs (Random Breath Tests): an on the spot roadside stop by police in which drivers are randomly selected to provide a sample of their breath to be tested for the presence of alcohol.

Reckon: think/figure/assume.

Red Frogs: Red Frogs Australia is a Christian Youth charity run by volunteers known as the 'Red Frogs Crew'. Also an Australian lolly that is red and looks like a frog.

Red Ps: the P1 provisional driving licence.

Rubber: an eraser.

Rugby League: a full-contact team sport played by two teams of 13 players. *Not* the sport known as 'rugby' overseas, which is known as rugby union in Australia. See also: **Rugby Union** and **NRL**.

Rugby Union: a full-contact team sport played by two teams of 15 players. This is the sport known as 'rugby' overseas. See also: **Rugby League**.

Rugging up: rug up = bundle up; to keep warm when it's cold outside.

Runners: abbreviation of running shoes, meaning sneakers.

Sanga: a sandwich.

Sausage sizzle: 'sausage in bread' or 'sausage sandwich', a grilled sausage in a piece of bread, usually served with tomato sauce and optional grilled onions.

SBS: Special Broadcasting Service, a hybrid-funded public service broadcaster with a mandate to provide multilingual and multicultural radio and television services.

Scab: in addition to common meanings (part of the body's healing or an insult to someone who crosses a strike picket line), also used in Australia as both a noun and verb for begging for food from a friend. For example, "Can I scab some of your chips?" or "She's such a scab."

Second Fleet: the second group of ships (with prisoners and supplies) sent from England to the colony in what is now Sydney. Consisted of six ships and arrived in 1790, two years after the first colonisers. See also: **First Fleet**.

Seppo: an American. A derogatory term short for "septic tank", rhyming slang for Yank. See also: **Yank**.

Servo: service station/petrol station. See also: **Petrol**.

She'll be right: it will be fine.

Shout: a round of drinks paid for by a particular person. See also: **My shout**.

Sickie: a day off work due to illness. Related to this is **Chuck a sickie**: to pretend to be sick to get a day off work.

Skull: to drink something quickly in one go.

Smoko: a short work break. Derived from 'smoke' as in a break to smoke a cigarette.

Snag: sausage.

Spud: potato.

Steve Irwin: Stephen Robert Irwin, nicknamed "The Crocodile Hunter", was an Australian zookeeper, conservationist, television personality, wildlife educator, and environmentalist. See also: **Crocodile Hunter**.

Straya: Australia.

Strine: Australian English.

Stubbie: a small bottle of beer.

Stubbies: short work shorts that men wear.

Stubby-holder: a cylindrical foam holder for your beer can, to keep it cool.

Sunnies: sunglasses.

Swag: a portable sleeping unit. Originally a bundle of belongings rolled up for easy carrying.

Swagman: a person carrying a swag or bundle of belongings while travelling on foot.

Swimmers: swimsuit. See also: **Bathers**, **Cossie**, **Togs**.

TAFE: Technical And Further Education, a government-run system that provides education after high school in trades (including study as part of apprenticeships) and vocational areas like beauty, design, childcare, accounting, business, recruitment, IT, and more.

Take the piss: make a joke about someone.

Tall poppy syndrome: a term that refers to successful people being criticised. This occurs when their peers believe they are too successful or are bragging about their success. Intense scrutiny and criticism of such a person is called "Cutting down the tall poppy".

Tax File number (TFN): your personal reference number in the tax and superannuation systems.

Thongs: a lightweight slip-on sandal with a Y-shaped strap (thong) stretching from between the big toe and second toe to the sides of the foot, and no heel strap. Also known in various places as pluggers, jandals, and flip-flops.

Togs: swimsuit. See also: **Bathers**, **Cossie**, **Swimmers**.

Tradie: short for tradesman. A skilled manual worker in a particular craft or trade.

Try-hard: someone annoyingly enthusiastic or who tries too much to please others.

U-ey: a U-turn – turning a vehicle 180 degrees.

Wag: skip class.

Walkabout: traditionally an Aboriginal rite of passage in which a youth would take a solo journey in the wilderness as part of a spiritual journey into adulthood. The term has been used to pejoratively characterise Australia's Indigenous peoples as unreliable, likely to wander off at any time. In modern usage, 'going walkabout' means to travel – something many Australians enjoy.

Whinge: to whine/complain. To "have a whinge" is slightly different, less like whining, more like venting.

Whinger: someone who whines/complains a lot.

Woop-Woop: an imaginary town, used to indicate a place far away/in the country.

Vegemite: a thick, dark spread extracted from the yeasty waste of the beer-brewing process, seasoned with celery, onion, salt, and some undisclosed extra flavours. As unappetising as that sounds, it is an Australian icon, and quite delicious when spread sparingly on hot buttered toast. (Similar to Marmite.)

Wallabies, The: Australia's national men's Rugby Union team. See also: **Rugby Union**.

Work experience: usually takes place in Year 10, and is designed to give students exposure to working life and insight into employment in a particular industry.

Yank: an American. A mildly derogatory term, creating the rhyming slang "septic tank". See also: **Seppo**.

Yeah, Nah: no. See also: **Nah, Yeah**.

Year 10 Formal: a school prom to celebrate the end of required schooling.

Year 12 Formal: a school prom to celebrate the end of secondary schooling.

Australia resources referred to in the text

ADF Careers/Education
https://www.adfcareers.gov.au/

Alcohol Information
https://www.health.gov.au/topics/alcohol

Apprenticeships
https://www.apprenticeships.gov.au/

Association of Social Workers
https://www.aasw.asn.au/find-a-social-worker

Australian Climate Service
https://www.acs.gov.au/pages/bushfires

Beyond Blue
https://www.beyondblue.org.au/

Bureau of Meteorology
http://www.bom.gov.au/

Bureau of Statistics
https://www.abs.gov.au/

Bushfire Information
https://knowledge.aidr.org.au/resources/bushfire/

Centrelink
https://www.servicesaustralia.gov.au/centrelink

Immigration and Citizenship
https://immi.homeaffairs.gov.au/

Department of Health
https://www.health.gov.au/

Electoral Commission
https://aec.gov.au/

Emergency Calls
https://www.acma.gov.au/emergency-calls

Emergency Services
https://www.triplezero.gov.au/triple-zero/regional-services

FEE-HELP
https://www.studyassist.gov.au/help-loans/fee-help

Headspace
https://headspace.org.au/

Head to Health
https://www.headtohealth.gov.au/

Is Australia as egalitarian as we think it is?
https://www.abc.net.au/news/2015-10-28/sheppard-is-australia-as-egalitarian-as-we-think-it-is/6889602

Resources

Lifeline
https://www.lifeline.org.au/

moodgym
https://moodgym.com.au/

myGov
https://my.gov.au/

National Disability Insurance Scheme (NDIS)
https://ndis.gov.au/

National Police Checks
https://www.afp.gov.au/what-we-do/national-police-checks

Notary Services
https://www.smartraveller.gov.au/consular-services/notarial-services

Parliamentary Education Office
https://peo.gov.au/

Passport Services
https://www.passports.gov.au/

SBS Cultural Atlas of Australia
https://culturalatlas.sbs.com.au/australian-culture

Smartraveller
https://www.smartraveller.gov.au/

TAFE
www.tafecourses.com.au

Tax Office
https://www.ato.gov.au/

Tertiary Education and Careers
https://www.yourcareer.gov.au/

Universities Admissions Centre
https://www.uac.edu.au/

UV Index
http://www.bom.gov.au/

Voting Explanation
https://aec.gov.au/learn/preferential-voting.htm

TCK Resources

We understand that this might be the first book about TCKs and international life that you've picked up. You might not have known before now that there were words to describe this lifestyle, let alone a whole community committed to supporting people like you, and families like yours. In this section we will introduce you to some tried and tested resources we recommend. There are services, podcasts, and books – with something for everyone.

Services

The following is a list of service providers, working in Australia or globally, with a range of offerings for globally mobile families and individuals of all ages. The range of services below includes both free and paid offerings, such as blogs, worksheets, social connections, informational workshops, TCK-informed counselling, targeted debriefing, and more. (*Indicates services that are specific to the Christian/missionary community.*)

Thongs or Flip-Flops?
thongsorflipflops.com
The website inspired by this book! We will keep adding to and updating this list of resources there, along with other content for Australian families living abroad.

Ignition Kids
ignitionkids.com
Kath Williams provides virtual and in-person debriefing and training services for TCKs and their parents/caregivers, mostly in Australia.

Resources

Tanya Crossman
tanyacrossman.com
Virtual workshops, blog posts, and other resources for parents, caregivers, and international educators.

TCK Training
tcktraining.com
Full range of virtual and in-person services for parents/caregivers of TCKs as well as organisations and Adult TCKs. Includes membership options giving access to the full catalogue.

Kaleidoscope
kldscp.org
A range of virtual TCK clubs for ages 7–16, plus additional services.

Expat Nest
expatnest.com
Virtual counselling for teens and adults offered in several languages by mental health professionals who have lived and understand the globally mobile life.

Truman Group
trumangroup.com
Virtual psychological care for expats without access to local resources. Services for children, teens, couples, and families – everything you could need – from therapists who have lived and understand the globally mobile life.

Linden Global Learning & Support
linden-education.com
Learning support and counselling for TCKs worldwide.

Among Worlds magazine
amongworlds.interactionintl.org
Online magazine which has become a blog, written by TCKs, for TCKs. A wide range of content with something for everyone.

Ute's International Lounge
utesinternationallounge.com
A great resource for parents of multilingual families. In particular, check out her recommended resource lists!

PEaCH
bilingualfamily.eu
Another good source of resources for multilingual parenting. Based in Europe but the resources are useful worldwide.

*Interwoven
interwovenglobal.com
Christian TCK content, created in Australia.

*Interaction
interactionintl.org
US-based service with a wide range of services for TCKs.

*Global Trellis
globaltrellis.com
Virtual workshops and other resources for missionaries.

*A Life Overseas
alifeoverseas.com
Blog collective for cross-cultural workers worldwide.

Podcasts

This is a list of podcasts for globally mobile families and individuals, with different styles aimed at different audiences. (*Indicates podcasts that are specific to the Christian/missionary community.*)

In Transit with Sundae Bean
https://www.sundaebean.com/in-transit/

Diesel & Clooney Unpack The World
https://blog.chris-o.com/category/podcast/

Resources

The Life of a Third Culture Kid therapist
https://shows.acast.com/explore-your-story

The Global Chatter
https://theblackexpat.com/the-global-chatter-podcast/

Two Fat Expat
https://www.twofatexpats.com/

The Lonely Diplomat
https://www.thelonelydiplomat.com/podcast

Love Your Expat Life
https://girafecoaching.com/podcast/

The Expat Mom
https://theexpatmom.com/podcast/

The Round Trip Stories Podcast
https://www.roundtripstories.com/

* Pondering Purple
https://michelephoenix.com/mk-tck-resources/podcast/

* Taking Route
https://www.takingroute.net/podcast

* The Clarity Podcast
https://the-clarity-podcast.captivate.fm/

Books

This is our largest resource section. We have broken this down into different categories so you can quickly find books that match your needs. There are books aimed at different age groups, books on parenting or educating TCKs, books specific to repatriation, and more. (*Indicates books that are specific to the Christian/missionary community.*)

General/Comprehensive TCK Books
- *Misunderstood: The Impact of Growing Up Overseas in the 21st Century* – Tanya Crossman (Summertime Publishing, 2016).
- *Third Culture Kids: Growing Up Among Worlds (3rd Edition)* – David Pollock, Ruth Van Reken, Michael Pollock (Nicholas Brealey Publishing, 2017).
- *Belonging Everywhere and Nowhere: Insights into Counselling the Globally Mobile* – Lois Bushong (Mango Tree Intercultural Services, 2013).
- *Third Culture Kids: A Gift to Care For* – Ulrika Ernvik (Familjeglädje, 2018).
- *Expat Teens Talk: Peers, Parents and Professionals offer support, advice and solutions in response to Expat Life challenges as shared by Expat Teens* – Lisa Pittman and Diana Smit (Summertime Publishing, 2012).

Parenting TCKs
- *Raising Up A Generation of Healthy Third Culture Kids* – Lauren Wells (Independently published, 2020).
- *This Messy Mobile Life* – Mariam Ottimofiore (Springtime Books, 2019).
- *Raising Global Teens* – Dr Anisha Abraham (Summertime Publishing, 2020).
- *Emotional Resilience and the Expat Child: practical storytelling techniques that will strengthen the global family* – Julia Simens (Summertime Publishing, 2012).
- *Raising Global Nomads: Parenting Abroad in an On-Demand World* – Robin Pascoe (Rrlj Investments Ltd, 2006).
- * *Serving Well* – Jonathan and Elizabeth Trotter (Resource Publications, 2019).

Repatriation
- *The Global Nomad's Guide to University Transition, 2nd Ed.* – Tina Quick (Tina L Quick, 2022).
- *The Re-entry Roadmap: Find Your Best Next Step After Living Abroad* – Cate Brubaker (Thinking Travel Press, 2018).
- *Arriving Well* – Cate Brubaker, Doreen Cumberford, Helen Watts (Kindle Direct Publishing, 2018).

- *The Art of Coming Home* – Craig Storti (Nicholas Brealey Publishing, 2001).
- **Navigating Global Transitions Again: A faith journey graduate planner* – Frances Early, Jeni Ward, Kath Williams (Mission Interlink, 2023).
- * *Looming Transitions* – Amy Young (CreateSpace Independent Publishing Platform, 2015).
- * *Returning Well: Your Guide to Thriving Back "Home" After Serving Cross-Culturally* – Melissa Chaplin (Newton Publishers, 2015).
- * *Burn-Up or Splash Down: surviving the culture shock of re-entry* – Marion Knell (IVP Books, 2007).
- * *Re-Entry: Making The Transition From Missions To Life At Home* – Peter Jordan (YWAM, 2013).

International Education
- *Safe Passage: how mobility affects people & what international schools should do about it* – Drs. Doug Ota (Summertime Publishing, 2016).
- *Growing Up in Transit: The Politics of Belonging at an International School* – Dr Danau Tanu (Berghahn Books, 2018).
- *Third Culture Kids: The Children of Educators in International Schools* – Dr Ettie Zilber (John Catt Educational Ltd, 2009).

Books for Adult TCKs
- *Unstacking Your Grief Tower* – Lauren Wells (Independently published, 2021).
- *Incredible Lives and the Courage to Live Them: Thoughts of a Third Culture Kid therapist* – Dr. Rachel Cason (Life Story Therapies, 2023).
- *Belonging Beyond Borders* – Megan Norton (Belonging Beyond Borders LLC, 2022).
- *Girl Uprooted: A Memoir* – Lena Lee (Little Koo Press, 2023).
- *Finding Home: Third Culture Kids in the World* – Rachel Pieh Jones (Independently published, 2019).
- *Between Worlds: Essays on Culture and Belonging* – Marilyn Gardner (Doorlight Publications, 2015).
- *Worlds Apart: A Third Culture Kid's Journey* – Marilyn Gardner (Doorlight Publications, 2018).

- *Home Keeps Moving* – Heidi Sand-Hart (McDougal Publishing Company, 2010).
- *Letters Never Sent* – Ruth Van Reken (Summertime Publishing, 2016).
- *Unrooted Childhood: Memoirs of Growing up Global* – Faith Eidse and Nina Sichel (Nicholas Brealey International, 2023).
- * *My Tethered Heart: A Memoir* – Zoe Doubt (Independently published, 2022).
- * *Passages Through Pakistan: An American Girl's Journey of Faith* – Marilyn Gardner (Doorlight Publications, 2017).

Books for Teen TCKs
- *Arrivals, Departures and the Adventures In-Between* – Chris O'Shaughnessy (Summertime Publishing, 2016).
- *The Third Culture Teen: Between Cultures, Between Life Stages* – Jiwon Lee (New Degree Press, 2020).
- *Dear Pakistan* – Rosanne Hawke (Rhiza Press, 2016).
- *Belly Dancing at the Bus Stop* – Sarah Turland (Initiate Media, 2018).
- *The Long Flight Home* – Simeon Harrar (Independently published, 2021).
- * *Hidden in My Heart: A TCK's Journey Through Cultural Transition* – Taylor Joy Murray (BottomLine Media, 2013).

Books for Tween TCKs
- *B at Home: Emma Moves Again* – Valerie Besanceney (Summertime Publishing, 2012).
- *See Ya Later, Allie Rader* – Emily Steele Jackson (Independently published, 2021).
- *Home, James* – Emily Steele Jackson (CreateSpace Independent Publishing Platform, 2018).

Books for Primary School TCKs
- *Slurping Soup And Other Confusions* – Tonges, Gemmer, Emich, Menezes, Willshire, Ahmad (Summertime Publishing, 2016).
- *The Kids' Guide To Living Abroad* – Martine Zoer (Foreign Service Youth Foundation, 2007).
- *Johnny & Joshua: Coming to Korea* – E.J. Asare (Esthere Jean, 2019).
- *Chopsticks from America* – Elaine Hosozawa-Nagano (Polychrome Pub Corp, 1994).

- *Sammy's Next Move* – Helen Maffini (CreateSpace Independent Publishing Platform, 2011).
- *The Mission of Detective Mike: Moving Abroad* – Simone Costa Eriksson (Summertime Publishing, 2010).
- *Patches: The Moving Bear* – Leah Moorfield Evans (CreateSpace Independent Publishing Platform, 2016).
- * *Swirly – Sara Saunders* (Review & Herald Pub Assn, 2012).
- * *Adelina Aviator* – Jessica Vana (Credo House Publishers, 2013).

Picture Books for TCKs
- *Life Without Nico* – Andrea Maturana (Kids Can Press, 2016).
- *When Africa Was Home* – Karen Lynn Williams (Scholastic, 1994).
- *Half A World Away* – Libby Gleeson (Arthur A. Levine Books, 2007).
- *Moving Planet Isn't Easy* – Catalina del Rio Faes (CreateSpace Independent Publishing Platform, 2012).
- *Ben Says Goodbye* – Sarah Ellis (Pajama Press, 2015).
- *The Way We Do It In Japan* – Geneva Cobb Iijima (Albert Whitman & Company, 2002).
- *Here I Am* – Patti Kim (Picture Window Books, 2015).
- *Ameya's Two Worlds* – Aditi Wardhan Singh (Raising World Children LLC, 2022).
- *Sparkles of Joy* – Aditi Wardhan Singh (Raising World Children LLC, 2020).
- * *Roses on Baker Street* – Eileen Berry (Bob Jones University Press, 1997).
- * *Jennifer of the Jungle* – Corbin Hillam (Concordia Pub House, 1990).

About the Authors

Tanya Crossman

Tanya Crossman is the Director of Research and International Education at TCK Training, a leading provider of preventive care, training and support for Third Culture Kids, parents/caregivers, and the organisations that send them overseas. She has mentored teens since 1999 and has 18 years' experience working with Third Culture Kids and globally mobile families. Tanya is known around the world for her writing and research, which explore the experiences of people raised internationally. She has delivered training workshops to groups in various sectors on five continents.

Tanya is the author of *Misunderstood: The Impact of Growing Up Overseas in the 21st Century* (2016) and lead author of three white papers: *Caution and Hope: The Prevalence of Adverse Childhood Experiences in Globally Mobile Third Culture Kids* (2022), *TCKs at Risk: Risk Factors and Risk Mitigation for Globally Mobile Families* (2022), and *Sources of Trauma in International Childhoods: Providing Individualized Support to Increase Positive Outcomes for Higher Risk Families* (2023), all available at tcktraining.com/research

Outside of work Tanya enjoys singing, painting, listening to music, reading fantasy and sci-fi, cooking Chinese food, indulging in Australian chocolate, watching TV with her husband, and bragging about/spoiling her eight nieces and nephews.

Learn more about Tanya:

Website: TanyaCrossman.com
Twitter: TanyaTCK
Facebook/Instagram: MisunderstoodTCK

Kath Williams

Kath is a professional social worker with an enduring passion for working alongside Third Culture Kids as they grow and develop and to see them thrive. She is currently employed as a Third Culture Kid Advocate by two mission organisations in Australia.

Kath has 20 years' experience working with children and teens, including working with Indigenous communities, foster children, and community campsites. She also spent two years in Cambodia, where she had a role in the student support team at Hope International School and volunteered at the local international church youth group with middle school and high school students.

When Kath is not working you can catch her going out for coffee and food with friends, exploring with her camera, going to any zoos she can, reading, listening to music, and travelling as much as she can.

Learn more about Kath:

Website: IgnitionKids.com
Facebook: IgnitionKids2023

www.ingramcontent.com/pod-product-compliance
Lightning Source LLC
Chambersburg PA
CBHW062050270326
41931CB00013B/3013